D1016574

Winning the
GAME OF THRONES

Other Works by Valerie Estelle Frankel

Henry Potty and the Pet Rock: An Unauthorized Harry Potter Parody

Henry Potty and the Deathly Paper Shortage: An Unauthorized Harry Potter Parody

Buffy and the Heroine's Journey

From Girl to Goddess: The Heroine's Journey in Myth and Legend

Katniss the Cattail: An Unauthorized Guide to Names and Symbols in The Hunger Games

The Many Faces of Katniss Everdeen: Exploring the Heroine of The Hunger Games

Harry Potter, Still Recruiting: An Inner Look at Harry Potter Fandom

An Unexpected Parody: The Unauthorized Spoof of The Hobbit Movie

Teaching with Harry Potter

Myths and Motifs in The Mortal Instruments

Winter is Coming: Symbols, Portents, and Hidden Meanings in A Game of Thrones

Winning the GAME OF THRONES

The Host of Characters and their Agendas

Valerie Estelle Frankel

Winning the Game of Thrones is an unauthorized guide and commentary on *A Game of Thrones* and its related book series. None of the individuals or companies associated with this book or television series or any merchandise based on this series has in any way sponsored, approved, endorsed, or authorized this book.

Copyright © 2013 Valerie Estelle Frankel
All rights reserved.

LITCRIT PRESS
ISBN-13: 978-0615817446
ISBN-10: 0615817440

With thanks to the many people who insisted I read this, I watch this, and I discuss this at parties and game nights. This includes my cousin David Kanter for giving me the first book well over a decade ago, my dad for flipping on an early episode when I came over and offering his hours and hours of comments on the shows, Matt Gottlieb for hosting the game nights and indulging my recent obsession with the series, Yonatan Bryant for introducing me to the *Game of Thrones* card game and having a conversation in Hodor-speak, and Ben Leitner for debating the series and offering opinions on my opinions as always. Without all of you, the book wouldn't be here.

CONTENTS

INTRODUCTION

A Game of Thrones is delighting a new group of fans, even as book lovers have been enjoying the series for decades. But its biggest downside onscreen is the enormous host of characters (far more enormous in the books – the fan-created wiki has over 5,000 pages). Too many times at parties I hear people wondering, "Who was that guy, you know, the one who works for Tyrion?" Or "Which one is he again?" The lengthy history of the Targaryens has been lost to television watchers, and with it the roots of the battle between fire and ice, as Old Nan's tales wake once more.

At parties, the fans demand to know how Robb could marry so foolishly, or wonder who destroyed Winterfell. Did Illyrio know what he was doing when he gave Daenerys exactly three dragon eggs? What are the Faceless Men plotting? Characters' motivations are messy, or sometimes hidden, from schemers like Varys or Tywin to pawns like Sansa and Ros.

And of course, there are the great mysteries of the series: Who is Jon's mother? What do the Others want? Who will Daenerys marry and what is the Targaryens' real gift? How will it all end?

This book is intended to help, exploring motivations and answering the fans' burning questions through deep character analysis, symbolism, and prophecy. Jon and Bran's classic hero journeys and Daenerys's heroine journey indicate where the characters are heading. A guide to people and places has been provided as well. All of the above focuses on events of the show, keeping free of dreaded "spoilers" and characters cut for time while nonetheless providing deeper insights from the books. Interviews with producers, actors, and Martin himself likewise aid in understanding the greater story.

Martin's characters are heavily based in British history, but with many nods to Rome, as well as myths from the Celts, Norse, and Greeks, and even the Bible. King Arthur and Robin Hood have their moments in Martin's saga, though no series more so than *The Lord of the Rings*. For fans reading the books, there are many more references, covering everything from *Conan the Barbarian* to *The Princess Bride*. Also, *Monty Python, Blackadder,* and *The Three Stooges* make appearances as Martin tests who's truly paying attention.

George Raymond Richard Martin has been called "the American Tolkien," and he's consistently on the *New York Times* Bestseller list, with millions sold. Along with *A Song of Ice and Fire* (the book series – *A Game of Thrones* is the title of book one) he edits the *Wild Card* anthologies and has written many science fiction, horror, and other short stories, many of which briefly appear in *Ice and Fire*.

Readers today eagerly anticipate the last two *Ice and Fire* books along with more short stories set in Westeros…the next of which is due to arrive December 2013. Between the books and show, this series is set to continue far into the future.

THE CHRONICLE OF THE TARGARYENS

The Loss of Valyria

In the ancient history of George R.R. Martin's world, the great empire of Valyria was the most advanced civilization of its time. It covered much of the eastern continent, Essos. Forty families strong in magic (including the Targaryens) ruled, conquering the known world. For some reason that remains a mystery, they colonized the isle of Dragonstone, but did not begin to conquer Westeros.

When most powerful, the Valyrian Freehold built all the current Free Cities (except Braavos). The Valyrians molded rock like clay to make ancient roads, as well as Dragonstone Castle, where Stannis now lives. With thousands of slaves, they excavated the Fourteen Flames, a great ring of volcanoes, for precious metals. About a hundred years before Aegon's Landing, when the first Targaryen dragon rider came to Westeros from across the sea, the land was suddenly destroyed.

Little is known of this event, referred to as the Doom of Valyria. A great (and unspecified) cataclysm that sounds much like a volcano fragmented the land into many islands. The area, called the Smoking Sea, is now described as "demon-haunted," and it is said, "The Doom still rules in Valyria" (V:73). Tyrion Lannister reads in his books that in a single day every hill for 500 miles split asunder to fill the air with ash and smoke and fire, blazes so hot and hungry that even flying dragons were engulfed and consumed. Great rents had opened in the earth, swallowing palaces, temples, entire towns. Lakes boiled or turned to acid, mountains burst, fiery fountains spewed molten rock a thousand feet into the air, red clouds rained down dragonglass and the black blood of demons, and to the north the ground splintered and collapsed and fell in on itself as an angry sea came rushing in. "The proudest city in all the world was gone in an instant, its fabled empire vanished in a day, the Lands of the Long Summer scorched and drowned and blighted" (V:446).

Dragons, which filled Valyria, are rumored to have originated in the Shadow Lands beyond Asshai to the southeast. The Valyrians learned to control them with magic and fashioned great horns of magic and Valyrian steel to become the dragons' masters. Aegon the Conqueror came from Valyria with his dragons, dragon horns, magic, and Valyrian steel, the secrets of all of which have been lost to time. But Old Valyria may hold the key to mankind's salvation.

Questions and Echoes:
- Valyria was destroyed by fire – likely a series of volcanic eruptions. It had much forgotten lore, from magical roads to the Valyrian steel and dragons that could fight the Others. Perhaps its fire magic holds the key to defeating the ice creatures. The Smoking Sea is a place of salt and smoke, like Dragonstone – the Lightbringer prophecy might take place at either.

● Tyrion puzzles why the Old Valyrians colonized the one island and nothing more, thinking, "Odd, that. Dragonstone is no more than a rock. The wealth was farther west, but they had dragons. Surely they knew that it was there" (V:76). Did Dragonstone give them exactly what they needed? Or did they fear the frozen Others?

● What magic is still waiting on Dragonstone and why hasn't Stannis discovered it? Martin comments, "If you look at how the citadel of Dragonstone was built and how in some of its structures the stone was shaped in some fashion with magic...yes, it's safe to say that there's something of Valyrian magic still present."[1]

● Is fire magic why Dragonstone called to the Valyrians? Or was it the volcanoes seething within?

● Already, there has been one apocalypse through ice – The Long Winter of Old Nan's tales – and one through fire. Now ice is beginning again. Is the Doom of Valyria significant? One curious fan asked Martin: "Was the Doom related to dragons, i.e., did the Valyrians lose control of some of the dragons, or was there some sort of civil war fought with dragons much like occurred later in Westeros?" He responded with a simple "No comment."[2] Since he commonly suggests that fans' particular exotic theories are unlikely to bear fruit, or responds to deep analysis by saying "Sometimes a cigar is just a cigar," there may be something here. In book four, it is suggested that the Faceless Men were involved in the Doom (IV:322). Their magic, like that of the Red Priests, seems unspecified but powerful.

● The Valyrians enslaved and terrorized the people of current-day Slaver's Bay. Daenerys's constant claims that she's descended from the dragon may be enraging the people of Essos more than ensuring their loyalty.

- Daenerys the Dreamer (ancestress of the current Daenerys) foresaw the Doom and convinced her father, the head of House Targaryen, to leave Valyria. They traveled to Dragonstone, and the Doom fell twelve years later. Of course, a second Doom may come. Daenerys notes in *A Dance with Dragons* that that the Dothraki sea is going dry and the grasses are dying. Perhaps the old world is burning once more.

- Six hundred years ago, Hardhome beyond the Wall exploded in what sounds like a volcanic eruption, or possibly the work of monsters. The "screaming caves" nearby seem to be "haunted by ghouls and demons and burning ghosts." Valyria's doom may already have been repeated (V:522). Was it a volcanic eruption? Or dragons, tunneling as we see Daenerys's dragon Viserion do? Or the firewyrms described as "boring" through soil and stone (IV:321)? The fabled Horn of Joramun, lost in the North, can allegedly awaken "giants from the earth" (II:276). Can it summon one or the other of these creatures? Or literal giants? Or volcanic eruptions that could bring down the Wall? All of these events killed many and devastated the land. Another such event may be coming…

- Valyria's destruction may have been caused by excess of fire and dragon magic. Now the world is threatened with ice. It may be a balance is needed to save the world from utter destruction.

Aegon the Conqueror

After the Doom, which killed most dragons in the world, the Targaryens still had three: Vhagar, Meraxes, and Balerion the Black Dread – the royal heads of House Targaryen rode them: Aegon the Conqueror on Balerion, with his sisters Visenya on Vhagar and Rhaenys on Meraxes. Arya mentions a particular admiration for the conquering princesses on their magical dragons, swords blazing.

Aegon the Conqueror apparently had never stepped foot on Westeros before the Landing. Like Daenerys, he was born on Dragonstone. He conquered Westeros with his sword Blackfyre and he had children with his sisters as their dragons did in the great Dragonpit of King's Landing. Aegon eventually conquered six of the kingdoms of Westeros and made peace with Dorne, the seventh. His dragonfire burned down the grand castle of Harrenhal and enemy armies alike. He converted to the Faith of the Seven and won the support of the High Septon in Oldtown. The high Septon prayed for seven days and nights in Oldtown and then anointed him, "For the Crone had lifted up her lamp to show him what lay ahead" (IV:421). Aegon founded King's Landing and forged the Iron Throne from the swords of those who surrendered to him.

Questions and Echoes:

- Daenerys names her ships for Aegon's dragons and likewise intends to arrive on Westeros and conquer it. She may need a Valyrian sword like Aegon's Blackfyre to be her Lightbringer or battle the Others.

- Aegon wed his sister Visenya, who was a warrior with a Valyrian steel sword called Dark Sister and gifts of sorcery. Jon Snow, a warrior of the Night's Watch with warg magic himself may echo her. If so, Daenerys may also need a softer man to finish her triad and ride her dragons. Aegon's other sister-wife, Rhaenys, was fun and playful, sensual and creative, with a love of music and poetry. Visenya crowned Aegon, and Rhaenys hailed him as king. The lords and knights cheered him but the small folk cheered the loudest.[3] All this may come to pass for Daenerys, without her conquering the kingdoms one by one as her ancestor did. But whom will she choose for her two companions?

Targaryen History

The Dance of Dragons

The Dance of Dragons was a major civil war. King Viserys I Targaryen raised his only child, Princess Rhaenyra, to inherit. However, he then married again and had two sons and a daughter. Under the law of male primogeniture as practiced throughout Westeros (but not in Dorne) Viserys was expected to name his eldest son heir, not his eldest child. The Seven Kingdoms divided between Queen Rhaenyra and King Aegon II. The Targaryen family itself became divided, and dragon-rider battled dragon-rider over Westeros. Many dragons and younger scions of House Targaryen were slain. When Aegon and Rhaenyra battled at last, his dragon swallowed her, though her son (also named Aegon) continued the war. Joffrey chortles about this while showing Margaery around the Sept on the show. When Aegon II finally died in battle, Aegon III, Rhaenyra's son, claimed the throne. The few remaining Targaryens and dragons after the war were sadly diminished. In Aegon III's time, the last dragon died. Martin's short stories note, "The summers have been shorter since the last dragon died, and the winters longer and crueler."[4]

Since this time, the Targaryens have not allowed queens to inherit the throne – with this policy in place, Daenerys could rule through her husband or son but not in her own right. (King Robert and the Small Council note that Daenerys is only a threat if she bears a son, specifically). Of course, between the shattered, warring kingdoms and her fierce dragons and Unsullied, the people of Westeros may not hold to this law.

The Blackfyre Rebellion

About a century before the series, Aegon IV, on his death, legitimized all his bastards and bestowed Aegon the Conqueror's sword Blackfyre on his bastard son Daemon (called the Black Dragon) instead of his trueborn son Daeron II (called the Red Dragon). "Some felt that the sword symbolized the monarchy, so the gift was the seed from which the Blackfyre Rebellions grew," Martin explains.[5] Daemon Blackfyre was joined by his half-brother, the bastard Aegor "Bittersteel" Rivers, while the bastard Brynden "Bloodraven" Rivers (named for his red birthmark like a raven) remained loyal to the King.

Finally, at the Battle of Redgrass Field, ten thousand men were killed including Daemon Blackfyre and his twin sons Aemon and Aegon. Bittersteel rallied the rebels and took out Bloodraven's eye. Bittersteel escaped to the Free Cities with the sword Blackfyre and started the mercenary group known as the Golden Company. When he died, they dipped his skull in gold, the first of many, and swore they'd bring him home one day.

Bloodraven with his Targaryen sword Dark Sister, and his destiny served as the king's spymaster for some time, famed for his warg-possessed "thousand eyes and one," that, like Varys' little birds, could be found spying in every corner of the kingdom. Later in life, Bloodraven joined the Night's Watch. He becomes a major plot point in *A Dance with Dragons,* as does the Golden Company…it seems this war is still being fought.

One year after the battle, King Daeron's sister Daenerys wed Prince Maron Martell, and Dorne entered the Seven Kingdoms. This Daenerys watched her children swimming in the Water Gardens of Dorne and realized common and royal were indistinguishable, all innocent and deserving of her protection. "It is an easy thing for the prince to call the spears, but in the end, the children pay the price" (V:510). Daenerys herself is learning this lesson across the sea in Slaver's Bay.

A decade later, Daemon's son, styling himself Daemon II Blackfyre, tried to raise a second rebellion, but Bloodraven, the king's spymaster, prevented him. Ser Duncan the Tall and his squire, Egg, got wind of the plot and fought to aid the crown. By this point, the sword Blackfyre had vanished. After, there were three further Blackfyre rebellions, before their house was at last wiped out. The last of these, called the War of the Ninepenny Kings (fought under Aegon V), included such fighters as Ser Barristan Selmy, Jon Arryn, and Brynden the Blackfish.

Questions and Echoes:

- The importance of Valyrian steel swords is emphasized here, of course. These swords may be able to kill the Others, to say nothing of being needed for the Lightbringer legend. Does either of these tales explain why they're so prized? What are their powers?

- Visenya, Aegon the Conqueror's older sister, wielded Dark Sister, a fact Arya specifically mentions on the show. Bloodraven inherited it and likely carried Dark Sister to the North. Perhaps he knew he'd need it more than the Targaryens.

- The Golden Company, formed of all the rebellious Targaryen bastards, still may have Blackfyre, sword of the king. If not, where is it? Will Daenerys, who's also in the east, take it from them? Will their Targaryen blood prove significant?

- What of Brightroar, the Lannister ancestral sword lost in Old Valyria?

- Why did Bloodraven join the Night's Watch? Was he curious about the White Walkers? Seeking the children of the forest? Or something else?

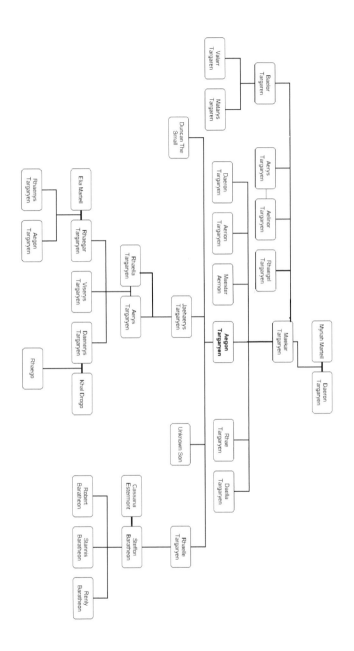

Dunk and Egg
Young Prince Aegon, fourth son of Prince Maekar, himself the fourth son of Daeron II (see above), attended the great tourney at Ashford. Seeking adventure, Aegon ran away from his drunken older brother and offered to be squire to an impoverished hedge knight, Ser Duncan the Tall. Ser Duncan was young and desperate to win his first tournament and establish himself, and he was persuaded to take on young "Egg," as the boy called himself. Ser Duncan ran afoul of a mad Targaryen prince, and after many events, Prince Maekar agreed to let his son travel with Ser Duncan and learn the ways of chivalry. Dunk and Egg journeyed from Dorne to Winterfell, in a series of highly beloved short stories by Martin. (The Hedge Knight, The Sworn Sword and The Mystery Knight, with others to come. These are available in various collections, listed in the Bibliography.)

When Maekar died, his two oldest sons had already perished, and the third, Aemon, had become a Maester (seen as the long-lived Maester Aemon on the Wall in Jon's time). Aegon took the throne as Aegon V, called "Aegon the Unlikely," as he had been so unlikely to inherit. He rained justly for twenty-six years with Ser Duncan the Tall as the Lord Commander of the Kingsguard. He had several children, including his daughter Rhaelle, who was grandmother to Robert Baratheon. In the third episode, writers dropped an Easter egg in for fans when Old Nan offers to tell Bran a story about Ser Duncan the Tall, adding "Those were always your favorites."

Summerhall
Believing a hot enough fire might hatch the last dragon eggs, Aegon V tested his theory at the Targaryen residence of Summerhall. In fact, the fire blazed out of control and Aegon V, his first son Prince Duncan the Small, and Ser Duncan the Tall were all killed in the blaze. In the chaos, his married grandchildren Rhaella and Aerys (later known as the Mad King) had a son they named Rhaegar. Summerhall would haunt the prince all his life. Aegon's second son Jaehaerys' reign only

lasted three years, and then *his* son, Aerys II, assumed the throne. (In a minor change from the books, Aerys II on the show is said to be the son of King Aegon V, rather than his grandson, simplifying the relationship between Maester Aemon and his nephew – not great-nephew – Mad King Aerys.)

Ser Barristan reflects that Daenerys's infatuation with a commoner is weakening her throne in the Free Cities, and compares it to all the doomed relationships of her family:

> Prince Rhaegar loved his Lady Lyanna, and thousands died for it. Daemon Blackfyre loved the first Daenerys, and rose in rebellion when denied her. Bittersteel and Bloodraven both loved Shiera Seastar, and the Seven Kingdoms bled. The Prince of Dragonflies [Prince Duncan] loved Jenny of Oldstones so much he cast aside a crown, and Westeros paid the bride price in corpses.

He ends by noting that treason and turmoil followed, "Ending at Summerhall in sorcery, fire, and grief." (V:875). Certainly, this cycle of history is repeating.

Rhaegar and the Trident

Aerys II grew increasingly mad after he was abducted during a brief uprising known as the Defiance of Duskendale. Barristan the Bold managed to rescue him, but the damage was done. In revenge for his Hand Tywin Lannister's uselessness (for during the siege, Tywin and his army had stood outside the gates, afraid to endanger the king by attacking), Aerys stole Tywin's heir Ser Jaime for his Kingsguard and rejected his sister Cersei's hand for his son Rhaegar, preferring Elia Martell of Dorne. Refusing to leave his castle, Aerys grew increasingly obsessed with fire, burning his subjects alive and commissioning thousands of jars of wildfire.

Prince Rhaegar, his father's heir, was obsessed with the prophecy that a great prince would be born of his parents' line. He named his son Aegon after Aegon the Conqueror and added, "What better name for a king?" On his birth, he pronounced, "He has a song…He is the prince that was promised, and his is the song of ice and fire" (II.701). He named his daughter for Aegon the Conqueror's sister-wife, and wanted a second daughter to complete the triad. When his wife only produced one sister for Aegon reborn, then was rendered infertile, Rhaegar began planning.

During the Tourney at Harrenhal, at which Ned Stark and his siblings met a young Howland Reed, Crown Prince Rhaegar offended Robert Baratheon by naming his betrothed, Lyanna Stark, as Queen of Love and Beauty.

> Ned remembered the moment when all the smiles died, when Prince Rhaegar Targaryen urged his horse past his own wife, the Dornish princess Elia Martell, to lay the queen of beauty's laurel in Lyanna's lap. He could see it still: a crown of winter roses, as blue as frost. (I:631)

When Rhaegar ran away to Dorne with Lyanna and hid with her in the Tower of Joy, her father Lord Rickard Stark and his heir Brandon Stark rode to King's Landing to protest and Aerys burned them alive while a horrified Ser Jaime watched. Aerys then demanded that Jon Arryn, Lord of the Eyrie, surrender his wards Robert Baratheon and Ned Stark for execution. This began a civil war.

House Tully joined the rebels, following the marriage of Ned and Jon to Catelyn and Lysa Tully respectively. Robert Baratheon killed Rhaegar in the Battle of the Trident, and with the death of the heir-apparent, the Targaryen supporters lost hope. Following this, Tywin Lannister, who had not declared himself during the conflict, rode to King's Landing. Unlike Varys, who counseled caution, Grand Maester Pycelle advised the mad king that Tywin could be trusted, and the gates were opened. Tywin Lannister then declared for Robert, sacked the city, and had his knights, led by Gregor Clegane, "the Mountain that Rides," murder Rhaegar's small children Rhaenys and Aegon, along with Rhaegar's wife Elia. Ser Jaime stabbed King Aerys in the back.

The pregnant Queen Rhaella and her small son Prince Viserys fled to Dragonstone, where Rhaella died giving birth to Princess Daenerys amidst salt and smoke. Her children were spirited to the Free Cities by the king's master-at-arms, Ser Willem Darry, but left to wander and seek wealthy friends after their guardian died. On the strength of his success in battle and his Targaryen grandmother, Robert Baratheon became king and wed Cersei Lannister. Jon Arryn became his Hand.

Of course, these events fuel the conflicts of the series, especially season one. All the adults remember the war, and Jon, Ned, and Robert's friendship was founded on it. Ser Barristan the Bold, Varys the Spymaster, Grand Maester Pycelle, and others worked for King Aerys before they transferred their loyalty to Robert. The mystery of Jon Snow's parentage, Jaime's legacy as Kingslayer, Cersei, Catelyn, and Lysa's political marriages all remain dangling threads woven into the tapestry of story.

The Saga Begins

A Game of Thrones (the novel) begins with the prologue of White Walkers attacking a few rangers, then the first chapter with the Stark children finding the direwolves after a deserting ranger's execution. The show starts the same way. Many wonder why we start after Robert's Rebellion, in a time of (temporary) peace. However, most books begin in a time of calm...moments before the epic struggle begins to unfold. The peace allows us to get to know characters slowly: First the Starks, then King Robert and his entourage, then the people of King's Landing and the larger world. Martin comments:

> I don't really remember why I decided that point; it probably wasn't a conscious decision. I mean, you are sitting down and you wait... the story just comes to you and you follow its needs. For me, the story started with the direwolves in the snow and that was the first chapter written; then I wrote the second and the prologue, which comes before all of that, was written later, so the first thing I actually wrote was that scene in the snow. Everything sets in motion from there.[6]

Thus the history of Westeros informs the actions of the characters, with old alliances and conflicts reaching through the ages to today.

YOU WIN OR YOU DIE: AGENDAS ON GAME OF THRONES

Most characters, from the Tyrells to the Baratheons, want power. In fact most characters are quite upfront about their agendas. Some of the coming-of-age stories – Daenerys, Jon, Robb, and Theon's arcs, for instance, are seen with them struggling between painful options as they choose what really matters. A few other characters are mysteries, leaving viewers divided on Varys' secret agenda or Sansa's perplexing words and actions. A deeper look, character by character, may offer clearer insight. (This is meant as character analysis – characters who offer startling spoiler-style revelations about who murdered who or what they've really been plotting are not included in this section.)

Petyr Baelish's Obsession

Petyr Baelish was born to an insignificant house on the smallest of the Fingers, hence his nickname Littlefinger. His father, a sellsword's grandson, befriended his liege lord Hoster Tully and

Petyr was sent to foster with him at Riverrun. Growing up alongside the lord's children, Catelyn, Lysa and Edmure, Petyr fell in love with Catelyn. This lady, however, was betrothed to her social equal, Brandon Stark, and chose the powerful lord her father had selected over her childhood friend. A jealous Petyr challenged the much older and larger Brandon to a duel for her hand. Beforehand, Catelyn begged her fiancé for Petyr's life, so Brandon only left him a scar and a lifelong sense of humiliation. Brandon was killed by King Aerys, and, while Petyr sent Catelyn a hopeful letter, she burned it unread and married Brandon's brother Ned.

Lysa in turn was in love with Petyr, and in the series, Petyr boasts around King's Landing that he had both Tully girls' maidenheads. After Lysa married Jon Arryn, she convinced her husband to give Petyr an appointment, and later to name him Master of Coin.

> Ten years ago, Jon Arryn had given him minor sinecure in customs, where Lord Petyr had soon distinguished himself by bringing in three times as much as any of the king's other collectors. King Robert had been a prodigious spender. A man like Petyr Baelish who had a gift for rubbing two golden dragons together and breeding a third, was invaluable to his Hand. Littlefinger's rise had been arrow swift. Within three years of coming to court he had been made master of coin and a member of the small council, and today the crown's revenues were ten times what they had under his predecessor...though the crown's debt had grown vast.

Petyr became indispensable to the crown, yet always overlooked and mocked for his birth. No one wanted him to wed their daughters or inherit their holdings, only watch the king's money. And so Petyr's resentment grew.

More than anything, Petyr Baelish wants respect from those who always sneered at him – in particular, he wants Catelyn Stark. His present-day actions all appear to be motivated toward winning back Cat or the nearest substitute.

Littlefinger befriends Ned and gives him a bewildering

mixture of good advice and bad. At last he betrays Ned to seize power but also to get Catelyn. His glee as he personally holds a knife to Ned's throat, the only time in the series he seems to get his hands dirty, emphasizes his agenda. He tries to have Ned sent to the Wall – with him giving up his lands and wife forever, Catelyn will be free to find another, but she won't be as distressed as she would be on his death. However, Joffrey kills Ned, and Catelyn is left to grieve. In season two, Petyr brings Catelyn her husband's bones and tries to persuade her to be with him. She's revolted and rejects him soundly.

Back in King's Landing, he offers to save Sansa and sneak her to safety. (In the books, Baelish also offers to take Sansa off the Lannisters' hands and wed her after her father's death. They refuse, for as Cersei thinks to herself, he's hardly of worthy birth.) In the later books, his actions toward her are a combination of affectionate and incestuously creepy. Sansa of course resembles her mother with shining red hair. She's an innocent seeking a protector – exactly what inflames Littlefinger the most. Petyr is also interested in wedding Lysa Arryn and inheriting her kingdom...but only after Cat refuses him.

He's also eager to be named Lord of Harrenhal – it's a vassal of the Tullys, but the Lannisters propose to make it the new Great House of the Riverlands – Cat's father and brother would be subject to Petyr, the poor ward they once judged not good enough for Cat. He could thus take his revenge on her family. In fact, since they're in rebellion against King Joffrey, Littlefinger could attack Riverrun and behead its lords if he desires.

On the show more than in the books, Petyr's center of power is the brothel, where he can order women to do anything he wishes – he will never be refused again. His whores on the show are an unsubtle means of controlling women...and notably, the red-headed Ros, with hair the color of Cat's, soon becomes his second in command. In the books, he "tutors" Jeyne Poole, Sansa's childhood friend, on how to please men within that brothel – since he cannot drag Sansa or Cat into his lair, he accepts a substitute.

Though Petyr seems to be a major player in the Game of

Thrones, his interests are selfish and petty – greed, lust, and revenge. As he gains more wealth and power, his fall seems inevitable.

What's Ned Hiding – Who's Jon Snow's Mother?

Three members of the Kingsguard: Ser Arthur Dayne, Ser Oswell Whent, and Lord Commander Gerold Hightower were mysteriously absent from the last battles of Robert's Rebellion. Ned Stark found them guarding the Tower of Joy in Dorne, where Rhaegar had spirited his sister Lyanna. Ned and his six companions, seeking Lyanna, battled the three knights of the Kingsguard there, and only Ned and his friend Howland Reed survived. Lyanna died in the tower, amid some amount of mystery. Ned Stark delivered Arthur Dayne's fabled sword to his sister, Ashara Dayne at Castle Starfall, and she killed herself from grief (again, under somewhat unclear circumstances and rumor). Ned rode home with the bastard baby Jon Snow to present to his young wife.

On the show, Ned identifies Jon's mother as "Wylla" when King Robert asks, but in the books it's much murkier: Catelyn guesses it's Lady Ashara, but Edric Dayne, Ashara and Arthur's young nephew, thinks Ashara's servant Wylla was the mother or at least the wetnurse (I:92, III:494). When Catelyn asks Ned about Ashara, he reacts badly:

> "Never ask me about Jon," he said, cold as ice. "He is my blood, and that is all you need to know. And now I will learn where you heard that name, my lady."
> She had pledged to obey; she told him; and from that day on, the whispering had stopped, and Ashara Dayne's name was never heard in Winterfell again. (I:65)

Wylla has told everyone at Starfall the child is hers, while it's kept a desperate secret at Winterfell, so it's likely she's not the mother. Ashara Dayne is dead, so if she's the mother, it's unclear why the secret is necessary.

The presence of half the Kingsguard at the Tower of Joy (with only Jaime left in King's Landing to defend the king and

Prince Rhegar's family) suggests they were protecting someone more important than their king or prince: their prince's prophesied child. Ned's constant thoughts about Lyanna's death also prove significant:

> He could still hear her at times. Promise me, she had cried, in a room that smelled of blood and roses. Promise me, Ned. The fever had taken her strength and her voice had been faint as a whisper, but when he gave his word, the fear had gone out of his sister's eyes. (I:43)

Blood and fever suggest death by childbirth, and the promise that haunts him would have to be caring for her child but telling no one who he is. By this time, Rhaegar was dead, and Robert had allowed the Targaryen children to be butchered as he sneered in contempt.

Jon resembles his father *and Lyanna*. (In the book, all of Ned and Catelyn's children resemble the red-headed Tullys except for Arya, who shares Ned and Jon's brown hair – and in fact fears she's a bastard because of this. Lyanna was so similar-looking to Arya that Bran confuses them in a vision.)

In the House of the Undying, Daenerys sees blue roses (Lyanna's favorite, symbolizing the unobtainable like Lyanna herself) blooming from an ice wall, hinting at Lyanna's child at the Wall (II:515-516). Further, Ned as he describes himself "had lived his lies for fourteen years, yet they still haunted him at night" (I:115). "The deceit made him feel soiled. *The lies we tell for love*, he thought. *May the gods forgive me* (I:504). Jon's mother is a *secret*, but it's only a *lie* if Jon is not Ned's son.

An honorable man doesn't cheat on his pregnant wife, but an honorable man would keep his promise to tell no one the truth about Jon, even if it destroys his family life, making Jon grow up surrounded by Catelyn's animosity. (In fact, Ned's inflexible honor often blinds him to the problems caused by his stubbornness).

Lyanna's death is romanticized heavily in book one, emphasizing her importance (while Ashara by contrast is only given a few sentences in any of the books). Lyanna, lovingly obsessed over by Robert and Ned alike, is thus revealed as key.

One pair of critics remarks:

> Robert's vision of Lyanna is bound up with the past, with his recollection of her beauty as he remembers it now. Eddard talks of her death, the details of which are vague but bring immediacy by putting the reader in the realm of the senses: a room smelling of "blood and roses"; the whisper of her voice as she pleaded; the clutch of her fingers; the dead, black hue of rose petals that fell from her fingers. The weight of tragedy and loss marking Eddard and Robert is palpable, bound in this shared sense of loss.[7]

Even Ned's brother and father are not described with this degree of love and value.

Of course, as a bastard, Jon is not heir to the Iron Throne any more than he is to Winterfell. With King Robert eager to kill the last of the Targaryens, Ned can be understood for letting Jon find safety and anonymity at the Wall if Rhaegar is his father. However, Jon's Targaryen magic and destiny may yet come into play. Martin only has revealed that eventually we'll learn the secret and discover who Jon truly is, and what he's meant to become.

What Is the Night Watch's True Mission?

"Make no mistake, good sers and valiant brothers, the war we've come to fight is no petty squabble over lands and honors. Ours is a war for life itself, and should we fail the world dies with us," Melisandre insists.

> All of them seemed surprised to hear Maester Aemon murmur, "It is the war for the dawn you speak of, my lady. But where is the prince that was promised?"
> "He stands before you," Melisandre declared, "though you do not have the eyes to see it. Stannis Baratheon is Azor Ahai come again, the warrior of fire." (III.884)

Certainly, those of the Watch must remember that their mission is not to battle wildlings (who are men like they are) but the wights and White Walkers against whom the Wall was built. Lord Commander Mormont asks Sam:

"If dragonglass daggers are what we need, why do we have only two of them? Every man on the Wall should be armed with one the day he says his words."

"We never knew..."

"We never knew! But we must have known once. The Night's Watch has forgotten its true purpose, Tarly. You don't build a wall seven hundred feet high to keep savages in skins from stealing women. The Wall was made to guard the realms of men ... and not against other men, which is all the wildlings are when you come right down to it. Too many years, Tarly, too many hundreds and thousands of years. We lost sight of the true enemy. And now he's here, but we don't know how to fight him. Is dragonglass made by dragons, as the smallfolk like to say?"

"The m-maesters think not," Sam stammered. "The maesters say it comes from the fires of the earth. They call it obsidian."

Mormont snorted. "They can call it lemon pie for all I care. If it kills as you claim, I want more of it." (III:451)

Have the ways of killing the White Walkers merely been lost to time as a thousand years pass? Or has someone helped the forgetting? Mormont notes that the children of the forest, who once brought the Watch a hundred dragonglass daggers each year, were killed by the First Men and then the Andals. Why? Weren't they on the same side? The children of the forest knew how to fight the Others and win. Likewise, the Maesters have aided the death of magic...they may have aided the forgetting as well. "The world the Citadel is building has no place in it for sorcery or prophecy or glass candles, much less for dragons," one says (IV.683). Long ago, their dragonglass candles allowed them to watch the world:

The sorcerers of the Freehold could see across mountains, seas, and deserts with one of these glass candles. They could enter a man's dreams and give him visions, and speak to one another half a world apart, seated before their candles. (IV:682)

The mysterious seer Quaithe tells Daenerys "the glass candles are burning" once more (V:152-153). Will the maesters offer their ancient knowledge and forgotten books to aid in the war? Or will they become a new fanatic faction determined to end the world rather than share it with another kind of belief?

Throughout time, the Night's Watch oath below has not changed, and within it may be keys to winning the war.

> Night gathers, and now my watch begins. It shall not end until my death. I shall take no wife, hold no lands, father no children. I shall wear no crowns and win no glory. I shall live and die at my post. I am the sword in the darkness. I am the watcher on the walls. I am the fire that burns against the cold, the light that brings the dawn, the horn that wakes the sleepers, the shield that guards the realms of men. I pledge my life and honor to the Night's Watch, for this night and all the nights to come. (I:522)

The war for the dawn, as Maester Aemon calls it, is coming, and the Watch must fight with light and fire (thus it seems likely the "Warrior of Fire" and wielder of Lightbringer that Melisandre foresees, the legendary hero Azor Ahai reborn, will be one of them.) The phrase "the sword in the darkness" also echoes this. Certainly, Melisandre thinks, "I pray for a glimpse of Azor Ahai, and R'hllor shows me only [Jon] Snow" (V:408), suggesting he will wield "the sword in the darkness," not Stannis.

"The horn that wakes the sleepers" is literally true as the men on the wall announce visitors with horn blowing. But the wildlings are questing for the Horn of Winter, the fabled Horn of Joramun, that can awaken "giants from the earth" and even tear down the Wall (II:276). Many believe the small horn Sam discovers in a box of dragonglass weapons on the Fist of the First Men is this horn. But if the rangers left it, it may be that rangers will need to use it – what kind of giants will they call forth for their war?

Why Did Benjen Join the Watch?

As Ned Stark tells Jon, Starks have served on the Wall through all their generations, as a proud duty. Certainly, Ned's younger brother Benjen wasn't required to take the Black, but he, like other Northerners, felt the southern lands could use his talents to protect them. Jon too is enthusiastic at the heroism of it all, before a few of Tyrion's remarks.

Of course, some fans suspect that Benjen felt guilty about what happened to Lyanna, in which he may have played a small part, even aiding her to joust as a mystery knight at the tournament where she was noticed by Prince Rhaegar. (Meera Reed tells this story to Bran – it's uncertain who the mystery knight in ill-matched armor was, but if it wasn't her father, it may have been the young and talented lady of Winterfell).

What's Sansa's Deal?

Sansa is the character many fans have trouble understanding. Season one, she was charmed by the handsome prince's choosing her above all others, sweet-talking her, and offering to make her the dazzling queen. But even as she deluded herself, the final episode left her betrayed as Joffrey valued cruelty over sparing her father.

The second episode heightens the contrast between the sisters: Arya names her wolf for the warrior queen Nymeria, Sansa names hers Lady – each wolf is named for who her owner wishes to become. In this episode, Sansa's flawed judgment becomes clear: Ser Ilyn and the Hound are monstrous because of their scarred faces. Joffrey the prince deserves her loyalty, for she is "his lady, his princess." This thought process of course results in the death of her wolf, Lady, and with her, Sansa's romanticized belief that handsome princes are always honorable and just. In the book, Sansa begins "crying herself to sleep at night," clearly mourning her lost illusions as well as her wolf (I:136-137). In this scene, Cersei and Joffrey literally kill Sansa's spirit, foreshadowing both killing her father in front of her and inflicting the slow emotional death that follows.

Some critics blame her parents for filling her head with tales of romance, but the loss of her wolf is significant. The wolves represent the children's' personal magic and power, the world of strength and otherworld magic they slowly explore as they learn.

In one blow, Sansa has lost all this. "If Lady was here, I would not be afraid," Sansa thinks much later (III:799). While her siblings are masks of civilization over growing wildness and warg magic, Sansa is only mask. As she imitates the queen's hairstyle in season one and Margaery's in season three, she demonstrates her obedience to the women who command her life.

In season two, she hates Joffrey and has seen that a flawed, scheming Cersei has no power as queen. Sophie Turner, her actress, says, "She was very vulnerable and naive, and now she's independent and has to survive in this world. That's a lot of pressure for a 13-year-old girl." Moving forward, "one of the main challenges is the mental and physical torture she's going to get from the Lannisters and all the people around her."[8] Logically, she might be trying to be a powerful queen someday and doing whatever she must to achieve it...but she's shown no sign that that's what she wants. And Cersei's example shows that Sansa won't really be a power in the kingdom, even as Joffrey's wife. She spends the second season acting cold in public and miserable in private. She doesn't seem to be plotting much of anything. The series has established that most characters are "playing the Game of Thrones" and seeking power. Is Sansa? She's not manipulating people to achieve her own goals, only acting to save others and convince everyone she's sweet and helpless.

She might be making the best of a bad situation. But that only makes sense if she has no other choice.

> Littlefinger: You have a tender heart just like your mother did at your age. I see so much of her in you. She was like a sister to me. For her sake, I'll help get you home.
> Sansa: King's Landing is my home now. (2.10)

Offered several opportunities to let strong, somewhat honorable men (namely Sandor Clegane and Petyr Baelish) escort her back to her family in season two, she refuses. Why? Every character has said she's in danger. She doesn't appear to being spying as Arya has been – she's never in important council meetings, only the public throne room. If she's loyal to the Starks, she should try to sneak back to them, but we haven't even seen her send a covert letter (which admittedly, could condemn her to death). Imagine how Catelyn will feel upon hearing that Sansa keeps refusing to leave, even with offers of safe passage.

Of course, Littlefinger has a somewhat slimy crush on Sansa, and strokes her shoulder during his invitation. Directly after that scene, there's one between Varys and a bruised Ros, in which Varys points out that Littlefinger exploits women rather than protecting them. Sansa may sense this or know that he betrayed her father to his death. Does she fear him too much to accept? Does she want to stay in King's Landing to play the Game? To stay protected as a valuable hostage?

The final possibility is that she's too scared or traumatized to act, even by running away, and possibly make things worse. She'd rather stand around, no longer queen-elect, and let Joffrey abuse her, rather than acting and possibly being executed as her father was. This is psychologically valid, especially with all she's been through, from losing her family one by one to her humiliations and injuries at Joffrey's hands. She's been taught that nice girls do embroidery, lead the women of the castle in hymns, nod and smile at the men, choose their words carefully, bear humiliation proudly. But this pattern of thought will only lead to a worse and worse life as she gives up her own happiness to be mistreated for the delight of others. If she's going to be anything other than an anti-feminist punching bag that the Lannisters degrade in every episode for her family's crimes and for being a "nice girl," she'll have to get mad. Or at least grow up.

In the book, the knight Sansa saves at season two's beginning pledges his loyalty. Though he's been made the king's jester, Ser Dontos finds ways to help her subtly and they meet in the Godswood. Their relationship is platonic, an image of courtly love in which the knight offers to lay down his life for his lady, and above all, to smuggle her home once they find the opportunity. Thus, in the book it's clear Sansa is biding her time until that comes. Her turning down more corrupt protectors makes sense, as she has her one true knight.

Season three emphasizes her status as desirable pawn – the Tyrells, the Lannisters, and Petyr Baelish all want her. With Sansa's passivity in this arena, as she mouths polite platitudes and refuses to accept or decline these matches, let alone make a run for it, she realizes she has no real choice – if Cersei, Joffrey, and Tywin decree her fate, or even chop her head off, she has no escape. And no one mentioned truly wants her for herself, only for the North. She has her scheme to marry Loras (in the book, it's his heterosexual, crippled elder brother, clearly trimmed to avoid unneeded characters). However, she modestly folds her hands and waits for Margaery to arrange it, not reflecting how precarious her situation is – after all, such a wedding could be arranged after she's safe with Robb and her mother. Her schemes, or rather, her agreeing to be a pawn in others' schemes, in fact come from a position of terrible weakness.

Many fantasy series feature the naive childlike protagonist, from Bilbo Baggins to Dorothy Gale. Martin subverts this by having most of his characters be quite worldly—those who are not die or quickly learn. Sansa cannot be the happily-ever-after princess, but she might absorb how to scheme. "Is it *all* lies, forever and ever, everyone and everything," a disillusioned Sansa finally asks (III:839). She's slowly learning that it is.

Nonetheless, it's worth noting that all the other characters around her "win" or "lose" – many in the Battle of Blackwater. Since the death of her father, Sansa doesn't noticeably do either. She pacifies, nods, smiles...and survives. "I am loyal to King Joffrey, my one true love," Sansa says, fully of dignity after Joffrey has had her beaten in public. Though she delivers the words with trembling and cringing sincerity before Joffrey, her words here have more than a touch of cold sarcasm when repeated to Tyrion. "Lady Stark, you may survive us yet," Tyrion observes (2.4). Like him, she knows when to keep silent and when to mouth off – when to lose her dignity and when to reclaim it. Like Tyrion, she's learned to survive in a world without allies. If she's killed, many fans would say she's had it coming a while, as she puts her trust in corrupt Littlefinger and Joffrey. But it would be a far more interesting story if she grows from naive captive to someone who can truly play the game, or who at least finds happiness with someone other than a handsome prince.

Why Is Brienne so Loyal to Renly?

A flashback in the books reveals this: When Renly Baratheon came through Tarth on a lord's progress, he was kind to an adolescent Brienne, dancing with her and treating her like a lady, rather than an ugly freak as most others did. At that time, she knew she wanted to spend her life in his service. He in turn, is struck by her desire to serve in contrast to his other knights' greed and ambition.

What Does Craster Do with the Sons?

As Jon discovers through spying, he sacrifices them to the White Walkers, who presumably make them into fellow undead creatures. (Craster's wives comment in book three that if Gilly and her baby don't flee, "his brothers" will come for them.) Because of this sacrifice, the walkers don't attack Craster, almost the only wildling who hasn't joined Mance Rayder. Along with demonstrating Craster's immorality, this subplot shows how desperate life is in the haunted North.

Who or What is Jaqen H'ghar?

The Faceless Men of Braavos are perfect assassins – for pay, they kill their target and usually make it look like an accident. They worship the Many-Faced God, whose watchwords are *valar morghulis*, "All men must die"; the formal response to this is *valar dohaeris*, or "All men must serve." (Both are episode titles.)

Jaqen is one of these men – when Arya frees him during a fire, he offers her three kills. He also offers her assassin training, though she must go to Braavos for it. Instead, Arya prefers to find her family. It's unclear how long he was in the dungeons of King's Landing, or whom precisely he murdered. He's seen in the fourth book, as his description matches the alchemist that meets the prologue character Pate in Oldtown (prologue and epilogue characters have grisly fates, like the Night's Watch deserter of the show's first scene or the elderly priest of the Seven who tries poisoning Melisandre.) Jaqen may even adopt Pate's face afterwards. It's unclear, however, what his new mission is.

Braavos is also the home of Arya's "dancing master," Syrio Forel, who most likely died defending her (his death is not certain, just likely). There's a popular fan theory that Jaqen was Syrio in disguise (suggesting the Faceless Men are so interested in season one Arya they'll send one of their own to train her at swordplay – a rather unlikely circumstance). This theory is complicated by the fact that Jaqen was certainly in the dungeons while Syrio was teaching Arya, excepting the possibility of face-switching. It's likely they were two different people and Syrio is dead. Jaqen, however, is alive and brimming with tricks.

Why Didn't Arya Kill Someone Important?

After Jaqen H'ghar offers to kill three people for her, Book Arya considers her options for a few days. She finally names Chiswyck, who led a gang rape. When the habitually cruel understeward strikes her, Arya names him, and his dog appears to tear out his throat. While considering a third name, Arya realizes she likely should have picked more powerful people. Her third name in book and movie is a clever trick – she names Jaqen in order to force his aid in saving her life. In the book, he helps her free the Northmen in the dungeon and stage an uprising.

Show Arya first names the Tickler, who has tortured many innocents, and nearly killed Arya's friend Gendry. Clearly the world would be better without him. In the following episode, she names the guard about to betray her to Tywin – this is treated as an emergency. When Tywin rides out, she insists that he must be killed right that instant. When told that is impossible, her next request is to allow her escape – perhaps she means to kill Tywin herself. When she names Jaqen to compel his help as she does on the show, he arranges an escape for her and her two best friends, though without the massive revolt.

In season three, Gendry asks the question most fans are dying to know – why didn't she name a major player? She could have ordered the death of Tywin, Joffrey, someone who mattered. Even her first "test case" could have been someone important.

On the show, Arya is rushed, and in the books, she feels she's been foolish in her modest choices. Besides that, the answer is complex. Arya is in fact a child – she knows the players but not the finer points of the war. Would killing Tywin help Robb? Possibly. But Robb is currently winning against the Lannisters, and if Tywin were taken out, someone worse, like Mad King Joffrey might get charge of the army. Besides, Arya has a sense of fair play and Tywin hasn't hurt her – in fact, he's been kind to her and to her friends. He's not on her personal attack list.

Nonetheless, Arya fingers a knife and stares at Tywin's bare neck on the show, wondering if she should – she can fight her own battles without the Faceless Man to help her. Certainly, Arya could have made her third name a deadly strike at someone like Joffrey, sacrificing herself in her brother's cause, but she's a survivor. Though she whispers names to herself at night, of those she intends revenge against, she appears to want to kill them herself. In fact, in the book, she's the one to kill the Tickler, as she stabs him repeatedly and sarcastically demands to know where gold and jewels are kept. Many fans were disappointed that scene won't take place.

> "Show me how – I want to be able to do it too," she tells Jaqen.
> "If you would learn you must come with me...The girl has many names on her lips: Cersei, Joffrey, Tywin Lannister, Ilyn Payne, the Hound. [In the book, she doesn't repeat Tywin's name, and she has several more minor characters on her list] Names to offer the red god. She could offer them all...one by one.
> "I want to but I can't. I need to find my brother and mother...and my sister." (2.10)

Arya wishes her enemies dead, but at her own hand, not that of a disinterested assassin. Only her need to save her family comes first. Once her family is taken care of, however, she holds the coin that will take her to train with the Faceless Men and see everyone who wronged her dead.

Like the Brotherhood Without Banners, Arya seems to

have appointed herself a champion of individual justice: Long after everyone has forgotten a single butcher's boy, killed on the king's orders, Arya is still repeating his name and determined to kill Joffrey, not for the good of the realm, but for murdering a single innocent. As she, like her sister, is disillusioned, she chooses not to pacify and be polite but to fight back for each individual. One critic notes:

> Mycah and Lady are killed almost as an afterthought, with nearly no effort being made to do what is just in the presence of the overwhelming power of the Iron Throne....A little girl, raised with illusions of justice and safety, must suddenly confront the reality of her world. Those in power, often with a thoughtless flick of the wrist, can destroy those things we hold most dear. It isn't long before trauma builds on trauma, as Arya witnesses the destruction of her family and the brutal execution of her father. Yoren may cover her eyes, but she knows what is happening.[9]

She responds to this injustice by righting it: kings and queens fill her vengeance list, along with the humblest of torturers and foot soldiers. As she recites them each night, she vows to bring justice to the world, man by man if she must.

Why Was the Freys' Bridge so Essential?

Robb Stark's host needed to go south towards Riverrun quickly to break Jamie Lannister's siege. The Freys' bridge was close, and going around to the south would expose them to Lannister troops and waste time they couldn't afford. Conquering the Freys or walking the long way round would take too long and expose them to danger.

> Theon shook his head. "The river's running high and fast. Ser Brynden says it can't be forded, not this far north."
> "I must have that crossing!" Robb declared, fuming. "Oh, our horses might be able to swim the river, I suppose, but not with armored men on their backs. We'd need to build rafts to pole our steel across, helms and mail and lances, and we don't have the trees for that. Or the time. Lord Tywin is marching north..." He balled his hand into a fist.

> "Lord Frey would be a fool to try and bar our way," Theon
> Greyjoy said with his customary easy confidence. "We have
> five times his numbers. You can take the Twins if you need
> to, Robb."
> "Not easily," Catelyn warned them, "and not in time. While
> you were mounting your siege, Tywin Lannister would bring
> up his host and assault you from the rear" (I:640-641)

Who Killed Jon Arryn and Attacked Bran?

Certainly, Cersei has the obvious motive for both. But the obvious is rarely what happens on the show. There are manipulative characters who say the right word in the right ear. There are petty, jealous characters who make bad political moves for personal reasons. Basically, there are murderers out there beyond the Lannisters.

The sheer number of players, especially in the books, makes the plot rather complex: Lysa Arryn's letter to the Starks accuses the Lannisters of her husband's murder. Then Jon Arryn's former squire, Ser Hugh, is conveniently killed by the Lannister knight Ser Gregor Clegane before he can offer any information. Much of Ned's quest is discovering Cersei's infidelity, which Jon Arryn uncovered just before he died. As such, the actual murder becomes secondary to him. Later, Grand Maester Pycelle confesses to Tyrion that he let the poisoned Lord Jon die to help the Lannisters. Basically, it becomes clear there's a massive conspiracy, even if some characters like Pycelle helped the murderer from afar. The murderer confesses to one of the main characters late in book three, so it's likely the real answer will be revealed in season four.

Bran's attack is nearly as convoluted. It's implied that though Jaime pushed him the first time, he's not the sort to hire assassins. The hired killer was given a rare dragonbone dagger, which Littlefinger tells Cat belonged to him, before he lost it to Tyrion in a tournament wager. After Cat kidnaps Tyrion and escalates the Lannister-Stark hostility, Tyrion reveals the dagger wasn't his – he never bets against Jaime. Tyrion also points out that only an idiot would use his own knife.

In fact, King Robert won the dagger in that wager and kept

it among his many weapons. One assumes he didn't arrange Bran's death, though he said in front of his family that it would be a kindness to end Bran's misery (On the show, Cersei inherits that line.) However, his armory was accessible to all of his household who traveled to Winterfell including the guards and trusted advisors. In Lysa Arryn's sky cell, Tyrion thinks to himself:

> If the old Hand had been murdered, it was deftly and subtly done. Men of his age died of sudden illness all the time. In contrast, sending some oaf with a stolen knife after Brandon Stark struck him as unbelievably clumsy. And wasn't that peculiar, come to think on it. (I:415)

He comes to the conclusion that he's being used in a conflict that's bigger than Stark and Lannister, and he also believes Bran and Jon Arryn had different assassins – someone is setting up his family. Even if Littlefinger didn't arrange the assassin, he set up Catelyn's attack on the Lannisters. Like the other murderer, Bran's attacker is revealed in the third book. So on both of these, just wait – it's coming.

What Does Melisandre Want?

> "He stands before you," Melisandre declared, "though you do not have the eyes to see it. Stannis Baratheon is Azor Ahai come again, the warrior of fire." (III:884)

Clearly she wants Stannis on the throne, or at least is aiming him that way. She seems to think he's Azor Ahai, the Lightbringer of the prophecy. She also wants to sacrifice those of royal blood to increase her own and possibly Stannis's power. She's a fanatic desperate to protect the world from darkness, though she may be misguided about the nature of that darkness…or she may be completely correct.

One problem is the red priests' inflexibility: Beloved characters like Jon and Sam are saved by the ravens and Heart Trees of the Old Gods, but Melisandre and Stannis go about burning the ancient groves, contributing, one must assume, to the power of evil in the world.

> There is no ambiguity about [other gods'] nature among the R'hllor priests. To them, the Others serve R'hllor's nemesis, the Great Other, reminiscent of the Christian split between God and Satan. The priest Moqorro explicitly says to the Ironborn, "Your Drowned God is a demon. [. . .] He is no more than a thrall of the Other, the dark god whose name must not be spoken" (*A Dance with Dragons*). To the Lord of Light's followers, all faiths but R'hllor represent the Great Other.[10]

With magic newly returned to the world, Melisandre may be a key player against the Other, or her inflexibility and fanaticism may doom everyone.

Martin tells us only, "Melisandre has gone to Stannis entirely on her own, and has her own agenda" rather than following the goal of the other red priests.[11] In fact, in the fifth book, the Maegi in Volantis believe Daenerys is the chosen one. What has Melisandre seen? Why does she pursue her own course? Possibilities include the following:

1. She honestly thinks she's found Azor Ahai and needs him to fight the darkness of the wights that are coming. It wouldn't be the first vision she's gotten wrong, as she misnames towers and characters – she sees the images but the meanings are often lost to her.
2. She has a crush on Stannis and is blinded by love for him, thus she thinks he's Azor Ahai and wants to have his shadow babies. (This seems unlikely – Stannis is the least charming person imaginable.)
3. Stannis is her power base while she waits for the conflict of ice and fire or the true hero. Possibly she's seen in her fires that she'll be needed in Westeros.
4. She wants something and being close to Stannis will get it for her – perhaps she's plundering Dragonstone for its ancient secrets or seeking the real Lightbringer sword.

A single, carefully-written chapter from her point of view in the fifth book fails to clarify much of anything. She has a vision of the past in which a woman cries, "Melony" and a man calls "Lot Seven," suggesting she was sold as a slave once (V:408). She believes she's doing the right thing to battle the darkness and protect her King Stannis. And she has a number of powers we haven't yet seen. Her story is still largely a mystery.

What Happened to Winterfell?

After Theon's emotional speech, his ironmen hit Theon on the head and leave for home – Robb promised amnesty to all but their leader. They're surrounded on all sides by the Bastard of Bolton's men – he's the son of Robb's bannerman, sent to save Winterfell and the Stark boys. When Bran and Rickon emerge from the crypts, their home has been burned to ruins. So who did it? Clearly the Bastard of Bolton. Why? Well, he's a sadist and a selfish monster, as we see as he takes Theon home to his dungeons. The books show him filled with a jealousy, ambition, and need to prove himself that somewhat echoes Theon's. Given the attack from a northern lord, perhaps it's less puzzling that Maester Luwin urges the boys to find Jon on the Wall, not seek out other northerners for aid.

Why is Tywin so Useless?

Tywin seems the Machiavellian mastermind behind the Lannisters. So why does he keep losing against Robb, letting Joffrey rule idiotically in King's Landing, and doing little else of use? Certainly his Lannister pride has led to arrogance. In season two, he, like many lords, is shocked by how well Robb is doing on campaign. As he struggles to modify his customary battle strategies, he's been seriously taken off guard. On the other hand, he's better in the council chamber than the battlefield. He notes that "some battles are won with swords and spears, others with quills and ravens" (III:260). In fact, most of his great plots work behind the scenes.

In the Battle of Blackwater, Tywin arranges the alliance with the Tyrells and their massive army after Renly's death and arrives at King's Landing in time to aid with the battle. Tywin's henchmen, like the Mountain that Rides, are terrorizing the Riverlands. In the books, he hires mercenaries to loot the Riverlands, but they desert to serve the Boltons (under the Starks) and savagely slice off Jaime's hand when they capture him. Ironically, Tywin has orchestrated his own son's maiming.

Season three Tywin returns to King's Landing and demotes Cersei and Tyrion for being incompetent (though this seems unfair in Tyrion's case.) There, a scene of chair-moving as the Small Council literally jostles for position seems his greatest accomplishment. However, many of his complex schemes from book three have not yet unfolded by that point. Basically, he's arranging covert and overt alliances, hoping that with a large enough army he can defeat Robb. His schemes in the book and show include having Littlefinger woo Lysa Arryn and her army, wedding Sansa Stark into the Lannisters (with Bran and Rickon allegedly killed by Theon, and Arya vanished, she's the only Stark heir after Robb), and even wedding Cersei off to Loras Tyrell. In the books, Princess Myrcella's betrothal to the Dornish prince is only the beginning of pacifying Dorne and somehow giving them Princess Elia of Dorne's killer (unfortunately, Tywin Lannister is known for giving that order) in order to get Dorne's massive armies. Going down the map, that's five of the Seven Kingdoms, leaving only one for Stannis, whose war grows ever-shakier. The last kingdom, the Riverlands, is in the worst shape, as the most fighting and sacking has been happening there. By contrast, Tywin can add Highgarden, Dorne, and the Vale – who haven't even lost troops yet – to the Crown lands and Lannister territories.

Further, Tywin's the source of Robb's two great betrayals, thanks to his "quills and ravens." In the books, Robb imprudently weds Jeyne Westerling, whose family are bannermen to the Lannisters. This proves more foolhardy than just angering the Freys – Tywin convinces Jeyne's parents to remain loyal to him and prevent their daughter from getting pregnant (with a TV wife from the Free Cities, it's unknown how much of this storyline will play out). He's also conspiring with a few of Robb's and Edmure Tully's bannermen, who eventually commit various treacheries and then declare for the Lannisters. Basically, most of Tywin's arrangements are quiet, underhanded work, withheld from viewers until they play out shockingly, but he's not just snoozing behind the Iron Throne. His plans to rein Joffrey in and teach him proper behavior are less clear, but he may feel they can wait until the war ends.

How Does Guest-Right Work?

In the most ancient times, enemies had to be set apart from friends – allowing someone into your house, past your walls, had to mean that neither guest nor host would kill anyone there. Bread and salt was a contract. It was similar to the Geneva Convention – everyone agreed on a set of rules, the breaking of which, like using chlorine gas or torture, was considered an inhumane breakdown of civilized life. In medieval times, travelers had to stay in fellow knights' castles or in inns. One might come down to dinner and find an enemy seated there already. Knowing there would be peace within the walls was vital, and losing that meant one's life would always be in danger.

In classical times, all strangers had the right to hospitality. Without even sharing their names, they were offered food, clothing, and gifts. Greek myth relies on this sacred law, and those who broke hospitality to attack a guest or host were cursed (this concept appears in the Iliad and Odyssey both). Zeus was called Zeus Xenios, guarantee of hospitality and protector of guests.

This tradition may seem extreme or outmoded to modern readers, but in ancient times it was incontrovertible for moral people. In the Bible, Lot is prepared to sacrifice his daughters to an angry mob rather than give them his guests, and Abraham makes a point of running down the road to beg every traveler to stop in for a meal. Middle Eastern tradition is clear on this issue, and even the captain of the forty thieves in *Arabian Nights* refuses to eat salt rather than accept this guest-right and then murder his host.

Europe of course has strong roots in the classical tradition. Dante's *Divine Comedy* names those who break guest-right the second worst kind of traitors, condemned to the lowest level of hell. *The Hobbit* references this trope – even irritating dwarves who show up from nowhere must be feasted. *The Count of Monte Cristo* refuses to eat in his enemy's house. *Macbeth* worries about killing his king, a guest in his castle, and certainly everything he does subsequently is cursed. *Ivanhoe* and *King Arthur*, especially *Gawain and the Green Knight,* use this concept. Basically, in classical, Biblical, and the medieval tradition founded on them, this really meant something. Parts of this tradition, like taking a fight outside the building where one is eating or staying, still remain.

So what are the consequences for betraying guest-right?

According to classical sources, as well as comments by *Ice and Fire* characters, those who do so are cursed forever by the gods. On a more practical level, someone who doesn't abide by the sacred laws has shown himself an outlaw, not a member of the community. Thus, no one will trust them, and others will feel free to betray hospitality to the oathbreakers. There's nowhere they'll be safe, and their most trusted friends may turn on them.

Where Did Daenerys's Eggs Come From?

Magister Illyrio introduces his gifts as "Dragon's eggs, from the Shadow Lands beyond Asshai." He adds, "The eons have turned them to stone, yet still they burn bright with beauty" (I:104). This is the land where the red priests originate and Bran has a vision of the country:

> He lifted his eyes and saw clear across the narrow sea, to the Free Cities and the green Dothraki sea and beyond, to Vaes Dothrak under its mountain, to the fabled lands of the Jade Sea, to Asshai by the Shadow, where dragons stirred beneath the sunrise. (I:136-137)

He may be seeing the past, or dragons may still exist, along with magic.

Dragon eggs appear to be like Valyrian steel weapons – hideously expensive, limited in numbers, but only somewhat rare in the east, more so in the west. Many fans wonder if Illyrio instead snuck the last few Targaryen eggs out of King's Landing. However, the scene where they're described in "The Mystery Knight" makes this unlikely as Egg (Aegon) Targaryen (great-grandfather of Daenerys) speaks to Ser Duncan the Tall:

> "I'd show you mine, ser, but it's at Summerhall."
> "Yours? Your dragon's egg?" Dunk frowned down at the boy, wondering if it was some jape. "Where did it come from?"
> "From a dragon, ser. They put it in my cradle."
> "Do you want a clout on the ear? There are no dragons."
> "No, but there are eggs. The last one left a clutch of five, and they have more on Dragonstone, old ones from before the Dance. My brothers all have them too. Aerion's looks like it's made of gold and silver, with veins of fire running through it. Mine is white and green, all swirly."[12]

Daenerys's eggs look noticeably different:

> One egg was a deep green, with burnished bronze flecks that came and went depending on how Daenerys turned it. Another was pale cream streaked with gold. The last was black, as black as a midnight sea, yet alive with scarlet ripples and swirls" (I:104).

And certainly, it would be easier to come across dragon eggs in Asshai. At the same time, the reference to ancient eggs waiting on Dragonstone may come to be important. The next section discusses why Illyrio may have chosen to give them to her.

Illyrio Mopatis and Varys the Spider

Contains mild spoilers concerning the introduction of a book five character.
The pair is hatching a complex scheme: It's revealed when Arya overhears them while "catching cats" in King's Landing that Illyrio and Varys have been collaborating for some time, though their goal remains unclear. Varys insists that he wants the good of the realm; however, his actions support a more specific agenda. As a eunuch, he appears to have less personal motivations than many – he has no family ties or grudges in Westeros, unlike almost every other character. Several characters

comment that it's impossible to tell what he wants. Illyrio arranges Daenerys and Drogo's marriage, but he too is a shadowy figure. Neither man is a point of view character, so every single thing they say could be a lie (though probably not the conspiracy discussion they share in the first book). Even judging them by their actions is problematic.

Oddly, the two strongest possibilities are that Illyrio and Varys want a non-magical, non-Targaryen puppet king who will let them rule however they like through him or that the pair has realized the Others are coming, and only real Targaryens with dragon magic can save the realm.

Varys was born a slave in Lys (according to Pycelle anyway). In the Free Cities, he traveled with a group of performers, who taught him much about disguises. However, a sorcerer of some sort offered the players a great deal of money for him and castrated him in a dark ritual; since then Varys has hated magic. (Varys tells Tyrion this in the second book. Tyrion notes that Varys' voice "was different somehow" during the telling, suggesting Varys is unusually telling the truth.) On the show, Varys follows this season three conversation by revealing he's captured the sorcerer and showing him to Tyrion. While this suggests the tale is true, it also reveals that Varys has many connections in the East and is perfectly willing to wait decades to enact revenge from a place of total safety and power. Retribution matters to him, but he has no need to rush.

According to Illyrio in the fifth book, Varys started thieving in Myr, and then fled to Pentos where he met Illyrio and they became partners: Varys would steal things and Illyrio would "arrange" their return for a price. This gradually changed from wealth to information, and both conspirators gained much money and influence.

Mad King Aerys, hearing about this amazing spy, recruited him. In King's Landing, Varys sowed dissension between his royal employer and his son Rhaegar, and Aerys grew more paranoid under his influence. Stannis reflects in the third book that "Ser Barristan once told me that the rot in King Aerys's reign began with Varys." Likewise Jaime tells Brienne that Aerys "saw traitors everywhere, and Varys was always there to point out any he might have missed." Varys alerted Aerys to the possibility that Rhaegar was recruiting allies against his father at the Tourney at Harrenhal (described on page 24), so Aerys attended, leaving the keep for the first time since his imprisonment at the Defiance of Duskendale. Rather than stabilizing the realm, Varys appears to have slowly unhinged it, or brought down the unfit ruler in preparation for another.

Why did he come to Westeros? Varys already had wealth and power in his homeland. Did he desire to play the Game of Thrones? Or did he have another agenda?

When Rhaegar had been defeated, everyone felt the Targaryens had lost the war from that moment on. Partially this was because much of the army died with Rhaegar but also because he was regarded as an excellent future king. With Rhaegar dead, Mad King Aerys lost his tempering influence, and the remaining heirs were tiny children. No one remained that anyone wanted for king.

Nonetheless Varys advised Aerys to bar the gates against Tywin Lannister, who came to "help" and instead butchered the Targaryens. Was Varys afraid for his own skin? Or was his loyalty to the king so great that he supported him even in inevitable defeat? Was he worried that the Lannisters would butcher all the Targaryens and their spymaster as well? This may have been a clever application of reverse psychology, but with only the facts provided, Varys may have actually been going down with King Aerys' doomed cause – an odd position for the intelligent spymaster to take.

Whatever his agenda, Varys then wheedled King Robert into leaving him spymaster, and as we finally learn, he and Illyrio set up a child to be raised as Prince Aegon, Aerys' infant son whom Varys allegedly smuggled from the castle before his death. (There's no proof whether the boy is who he claims.) In the fifth book, Varys and Illyrio both appear to want this boy on the throne (making this a long game indeed).

One possible but far-fetched motivation is that Illyrio and Varys, advised by Illyrio's red priest friends (Illyrio swears by the Lord of Light), learn that according to prophecy, three

Targaryen heroes will be needed to fight the Others. Illyrio comments in book five that the dragon has three heads – he knows the prophecy. Perhaps Illyrio even gave Daenerys exactly three eggs because he hoped she'd hatch them and find dragonriders. In this case Varys, needing a real Targaryen, protected Mad King Aerys and his infant grandchildren as much as possible. It also suggests Varys might have rescued the actual infant Aegon since he would be needed someday.

However, there are many problems with this: In fact, Illyrio and Varys let Viserys and Daenerys wander as beggars for a decade when they easily could have offered them more help. If Varys doesn't value those young Targaryens, he likely doesn't care about preserving a real Targaryen prince when any silver-haired baby would do.

After decades of scheming, Illyrio brokers the marriage between Daenerys and Drogo and gives them the dragon eggs, which he says he obtained from the Shadow Lands. Their hatching was not predicted by anyone – it's that shocking and unprecedented for the people of Martin's world. There are seers and prophecies around, certainly, but it's unclear how well red priests could see the future before Daenerys's dragon hatching brought magic back to the world. Most likely, Illyrio gave Daenerys the eggs because they were an expensive, purposeless status symbol. In Daenerys's thoughts, she explains, "It was a truly magnificent gift, though she knew that Illyrio could afford to be lavish. He had collected a fortune in horses and slaves for his part in selling her to Khal Drogo." Certainly destiny may have taken a hand, but there's no real indicator Illyrio gave her the eggs with a purpose.

The gift might also be interpreted as "Look, I'm honoring you and calling you a true Targaryen, heir to these eggs…then secretly sending you off to die." Illyrio later explains that Daenerys wasn't expected to survive – a thirteen-year-old sheltered, naive princess wed to the powerful khal and hauled into the desert? Little surprise Illyrio thought that. The scheme of marrying her off would eliminate Daenerys – as they think, an untutored maiden with Targaryen blood. She could not inherit in her own right, and the Dothraki would have no interest in conquering Westeros. The throne would be left for Aegon. Having the Dothraki honor the egotistical and mad Viserys enough to give him a Dothraki army and sail across the sea they loathe so much is a far-fetched plan compared with setting Viserys up to be overbearingly arrogant until they kill him – which is exactly what happens. Illyrio tells Viserys Khal Drogo will give him an army, and then sends the unhinged, bratty king off with the Dothraki without even giving him a courtesy lesson. Viserys, like his sister, was set up to die.

If Varys and Illyrio wanted the Targaryen siblings killed, Illyrio could have simply poisoned their dinner. A more likely and complex plot is that Daenerys's wedding was arranged to frighten Westeros and begin the panic and civil war that in fact resulted. Sending the Targaryen heirs off with the Dothraki, and reporting Daenerys's marriage and pregnancy to King Robert, as Varys does, gives Robert an excuse to send assassins and spiral into paranoia as Aerys once did. In the discussion, Varys urges Robert to send an assassin and tells Ned that leaders must do "vile things" to preserve their realms. Of course, the hapless assassin inflames the conflict further.

Around this time, Varys meets Illyrio beneath the Red Keep and Arya overhears the following fragments of conversation. (Martin has confirmed that the book characters she doesn't recognize are these two, and they appear as themselves on the show).

Varys: "I warn you, the wolf and lion will soon be at each other's throats, whether we will it or no."
Illyrio: "What good is war now? We are not ready. Delay."
...
[Illyrio suggests stalling by killing Eddard Stark.]
    "If one Hand can die, why not a second…You have danced the dance before."
    "Before is not now, and this Hand is not the other."
    "Nonetheless, we must have time. The princess is with child. The khal will not bestir himself until his son is born. You know how they are, these savages."
    "If he does not bestir himself soon, it may be too late. This is no longer a game for two players if it ever was. Stannis Baratheon and Lysa Arryn have fled beyond my reach, and

the whispers say they are gathering swords about them."
(I:343-344)

Varys goes on to list other families like the Tyrells who are scheming for power, and then asks for more money and more "little birds," child spies he can train.

A few facts are apparent: Varys and Illyrio are scheming for a Lannister-Stark civil war, but not until the time is right. Drogo and his army won't move on Westeros yet, and Varys and Illyrio need more time to organize their schemes. There's no mention of the Dothraki reaching Westeros, only beginning to march (and presumably take slaves and assemble ships). All this would throw Westeros into panic, a goal the conspirators desire. Varys doesn't want a strong kingdom uniting against a Dothraki horde, but instead a scattering of kings all fighting for dominance, some of whom might ally with Daenerys. They want chaos.

The conversation also reveals that Varys once killed a Hand or did something similar. Varys may have decided not to interfere with Jon Arryn's death, as he needed the Lannisters strong without Cersei banished or executed. Illyrio may also be referring to Varys' games in Aerys' court, where Aerys went through several Hands. Tywin was the King's Hand then before a paranoid Aerys fired him. Did Varys help arrange this?

"This is no longer a game for two players" is intriguing. Are Varys and Illyrio uniting against some other mastermind more devious and powerful than Littlefinger? (Tywin, who has all his enemies killed with a flick of his pen and has been playing for decades seems logical.) Is this a reference to the Lord of Light versus the Other? Or do they just mean it won't be a civil war of two sides but five? The sentence that follows suggests the last option.

During the first season, Varys drops hints to Ned that the Lannisters killed Jon Arryn and that the queen and Lancel killed King Robert, likely to encourage the Stark-Lannister conflict. Later, he convinces Ned to publicly repent his war against the Lannisters and make peace between the families, delaying the civil war. However, Joffrey unexpectedly kills him. Civil war begins, sooner than the conspirators planned. Then another startling event happens as Daenerys births her dragons out of stone. Suddenly, the young marriage pawn has become an important player.

After this, the conspiring pair take a larger interest in Daenerys. Varys suggests King Joffrey dismiss Ser Barristan Selmy. When Joffrey does, Illyrio sends Ser Barristan to join Daenerys. (In any case, Ser Barristan is a voice of reason in court, so he must go.) Likewise Illyrio provides Daenerys with ships and gifts. When asked why much later, Illyrio says, "Not all that a man does is done for gain. Believe as you wish, but even fat old fools like me have friends, and debts of affection to repay." This debt might be to Daenerys...but what did she ever do for him? Varys, who grew up with Illyrio and made him who he is, is a more logical choice.

There's an intriguing interchange between television Tyrion and Varys on the eve of Blackwater Bay.

> Tyrion: What do you want? Tell me.
> Varys: If we're going to play, you'll have to start.

Tyrion does, describing much about how he enjoys the power he'd never dreamed of having. This conversation drifts into one about the gods. Then Varys pauses, indicating a topic shift, which the following is:

> Varys: This morning, I heard a song all the way from Qarth, beyond the red wastes. Daenerys Targaryen lives.

They chat a bit about her half-grown dragons. Then Tyrion points out that Stannis is about to attack and adds that they must play "one game at a time." (2.8). Did Varys actually confide in Tyrion? Tell him honestly what he wants? (The fact that Daenerys is alive, with dragons, is common knowledge, but in context it may be Varys' answer, or at least the only answer he's willing to risk: He supports the Targaryens, both known and hidden.)

Varys claims that the purpose of his machinations is not for personal power, honor, or loyalty, but simply the best intentions for the realm as a whole. After his support of Mad King Aerys, this seems unlikely. In fact, he goes on to destabilize the realm and prolong the conflict until the right time.

A possible right time could be young Aegon arriving as savior. (Of course, if Varys is destabilizing the realm and Illyrio returns with a deliverer, they're playing the same game they played in Pentos in their youth.) While the civil war, lengthened by Varys, is threatening starvation, this only adds to the people's misery under all the Westeros kings. Illyrio notes: "There is no peace in Westeros, no justice, no faith…and soon enough, no food. When men are starving and sick of fear, they look for a savior…A savior comes from across the sea to bind up the wounds of Westeros" (V:30). This would pave the way for Varys' puppet king to arrive and bring peace and justice.

After book one, Varys continues to mess with Lannisters, helping and hurting Tywin, Tyrion, and Kevan along with Pycelle to further destabilize the realm. In book five, Illyrio begins young Aegon's campaign for power. Illyrio and Varys enlist the aid of the Golden Company of mercenaries to help. The Golden Company was founded by the Blackfyres, a group of Targaryen bastards who tried to seize the throne *five separate times* about a century before King Robert. (They feature in various flashbacks described pages 18-19 as well as the Dunk and Egg stories.) At last, the male line (specifically) was entirely killed off. In the year 2000, a decade before book five's release, Martin wrote, "The Golden Company is the largest and most famous, founded by one of Aegon the Unworthy's bastards. You won't meet them until A DANCE WITH DRAGONS."[13] Clearly the Golden Company is integral to Martin's storyline.

Illyrio notes that the company broke a different contract and signed up because "Some contracts are writ in ink, and some in blood." If Aegon is actually one of their descendants through the female line, they might be eager to topple both legitimate Targaryens and the pretender kings. While the company once refused to help Viserys reclaim the throne, defending their own may have always been their plan.

Why is Varys so desperate for his chosen heir to take the throne? This has required about twenty years of labor, to say nothing of countless deaths and the destruction of good rulers as well as bad ones. This preference for Aegon over Daenerys and her brother suggests that Aegon as a person matters to them, or that Varys wants the satisfaction of creating an able, non-Targaryen heir, not a mad, magic-using Targaryen. That being said, Viserys showed signs of instability and madness even as a child, while women are forbidden to rule in their own right. Only once Daenerys has dragons does she become valuable – with them, she's the most "worthy" Targaryen in the people's eyes. Wedding her to Aegon will solidify their joint claim.

Several theories behind Aegon's backstory are floating around online:

1. Aegon's an actual Targaryen, needed because Winter is Coming. He will be one of the three heads of the dragon and possibly Daenerys's husband.

However, most fans are skeptical that the hero who will save everyone is not Jon, Daenerys, or Bran but a new character introduced as late as book five. There are several prophecies of a false dragon or mummer's dragon that particularly cast doubt on Aegon. His traveling with a "halfmaester" and a false Septa emphasizes this as well. The classic Targaryen look is "silver-gold hair" and "purple eyes" like Daenerys's in the books (I:34). Aegon has silvery hair, but this is common in Volantis. His eyes are a lighter color than the deep Targaryen purple of Prince Rhaegar and Daenerys. Of course, if he's legitimate but gets killed or refuses the throne, the story arc won't be severely affected.

2. Most fans prefer the theories that he's not Aegon Targaryen but is in fact

    a) A descendant of the Targaryen bastards who founded the Golden Company and Varys owes them something or is a descendant of theirs who's concealing his silvery hair with his baldness. (He's spent the entire series as the observer with no family agendas, so this would be something of a disappointment.)

b) A descendent of the mad, savage Prince Aerion from "The Hedge Knight," who traveled to the east a century ago.

c) Illyrio's beloved son by his wife who had "pale golden hair streaked by silver," making him the schemers' adored family but not actually royal. (Of course, Illyrio's wife could be a Targaryen descendent through the Golden Company. Illyrio notably turned down better matches to wed her.)

d) A random baby from the silver-haired descendants of Old Volantis – Varys wants to *make* a good king, not watch one inherit because of an unstable, inbred bloodline. His hatred of magic and rough upbringing on the streets would support this.

Illyrio appears to care for the boy, sending him gifts and asking to see him before the conquest. Besides, the child, Targaryen or not, has been raised to Illyrio's and Varys' secret agenda and will show them personal loyalty. The three of them could rule the kingdom. In one scene, Varys describes needing the right king, not just the heir:

> He is here. Aegon has been shaped for rule since before he could walk. He has been trained in arms, as befits a knight to be, but that was not the end of his education. He reads and writes, he speaks several tongues, he has studied history and law and poetry. A septa has instructed him in the mysteries of the Faith since he was old enough to understand them. He has lived with fisherfolk, worked with his hands, swum in rivers and mended nets and learned to wash his own clothes at need. He can fish and cook and bind up a wound, he knows what it is like to be hungry, to be hunted, to be afraid...Aegon knows that kingship is his duty, that a king must put his people first, and live and rule for them. (V:958-959)

All this emphasis on his upbringing rather than his birthright suggests Aegon has been trained for kingship, not simply bred for it.

In summary, Varys seems to aid the following:

❖ Mad King Aerys (at least to increase his paranoia and dependency)
❖ Daenerys (only after she has dragons)
❖ His own young Aegon – real or fake
❖ A Lannister-Stark war (under the right conditions and timing)

On the surface, Varys seems to want Targaryen rule. But why? He's from Lys, where he became a powerful master of secrets before Aerys recruited him. Perhaps Varys wants to install a puppet king on the throne. Or perhaps he knows the war is coming and the people of Westeros will need a Targaryen. Time will tell.

OTHER FAN QUESTIONS

Where Can I Find More Books like Martin's?

Martin's other large series, *Wild Cards*, has little relation to Ice and Fire. A few of his stories, however, anticipate or explore issues later brought into *A Song of Ice and Fire* – writing doesn't take place in a vacuum.

For instance, Martin's earliest fantasy story sold was "Dark Gods of Kor-Yuban." In a sword-and-sorcery, Conan-the-Barbarian-style saga, the exiled Prince R'hllor of Raugg and his boisterous, swaggering companion Argilac the Arrogant travel the world. In a sequel, they team up with Barron, the Bloody Blade of the Dothrak Empire, to slay the winged demons who killed Barron's grandfather Barristan the Bold.[14] Of course, all these names appear in Westeros (even Argilac the Arrogant, who was the last Storm King overthrown by the Targaryens). Writers' ideas linger – they don't just vanish. His Dunk and Egg stories, listed in the bibliography, are direct prequels to the series, but for fans who can't get enough, the following stories may also be of interest:

"The Ice Dragon"
"The Ice Dragon" available in Martin's *Dreamsongs: Volume I* (Bantam Books, 2012) and as a standalone children's book may be the closest. This story features a girl living in a medieval world of dragonriders that could be Westeros. She befriends an ice dragon and uses him to fight in their war. Ice dragons have been mentioned in *Ice and Fire,* and this book only lends fuel to readers' speculations.

"A Song for Lya"
The Hugo Award winning "A Song for Lya" is available in the collection of that name and in *Dreamsongs Volume 1.* This novella features a tragic love story...the heroine is even named Lyanna! As she and her boyfriend struggle with romance and the meaningful questions of life, they touch on many *Game of Thrones* themes, like acts that can truly change a person, love, faith, and the nature of religion.

Windhaven by George R.R. Martin and Lisa Tuttle
Windhaven shares many of *Game of Thrones'* trappings. In a fantasy world of ballads, ships, and heroes, a girl longs to fly – not on dragons but on metal wings. However she's denied them in favor of her half-brother. As Maris (a name repeated in *Ice and Fire*) competes, she's proving she's as good as those born to the birthright. It also led to Martin's most beloved character. Martin notes:

> In 1981 I wrote a novel with Lisa Tuttle called Windhaven. In fact, we wrote three different short stories with the same main character, Maris, and once we had them written we decided to put them all into one book with three different parts. So while we were writing the books we thought about a dwarf who would have been the Lord of one of the islands. He had to be the ugliest person in the world but the most intelligent too. I kept that idea in my mind and it reappeared to me when I was starting to write Game of Thrones. So...That's Tyrion Lannister.[15]

Other Authors

Of course, readers looking for more books in this style could read Martin's favorites, both fantasy and historical. Martin said:

> I really like the young fantasy authors out there; they are doing some terrific work. I really like the work of my friend Daniel Abraham, who's just started a new fantasy series with The Dragon's Path and already has written a terrific one called The Long Price Quartet. I think Joe Abercrombie is doing some terrific work. I love Scott Lynch's Locke Lamora series. So those are three right there that they can take a look at.
>
> I also think that fantasy fans should go back and read the classics: obviously Tolkien if you haven't read him, but also works like Fritz Leiber's classic Fahfrd and the Grey Mousers stories; the original Conan stories by Robert E. Howard and his other characters like Bran Mak Morn and Solomon Kane; Jack Vance, one of my all-time favorites, the marvelous The Dying Earth stories by Jack Vance. We just did a tribute anthology to him just a couple years ago called Songs of the Dying Earth. Original Dying Earth stories written by old fantasy writers who were shaped and influenced by Jack Vance's classic stuff...Oh and Roger Zelazny. Nine Princes in Amber. I mean that's an all-time classic. They should definitely read those. [...][16]
>
> Also, I read a lot of historical fiction, both the classic writers of historical fiction that I read many decades ago – people like Thomas B. Costain and Frank Yerby and so forth – and some of the more contemporary writers of historical fiction, like Bernard Cornwell, Sharon Kay Penman, and Philippa Gregory.[17]

It's been noted that Martin's work fits smoothly among the most popular of high fantasy series, drawing on what came before and creating a standard for what came after:

> Just as he followed in the footsteps of J.R.R. Tolkien, Stephen R. Donaldson, and more contemporary fantasists such as Robert Jordan and Tad Williams, other authors have been influenced in turn by the [gritty and realistic] traits that Martin's readers associate with his series of novels.[18]

Along with historical fiction, many fantasy epics are celebrated for their politics and complexity. For those interested in political machinations (along with quite a bit of nudity) the *Kushiel's Legacy* series by Jacqueline Carey guides readers through a fantastical Europe as a courtesan struggles to save the realm from its own clash of kings. For historical novels reimagining the great epics, Parke Godwin has done excellent takes on Robin Hood, King Arthur, and so forth, set in historical England. *The Secret Texts* by Holly Lisle introduces feuding houses in which even the worst villains have their moral complexity. Like Martin, Lisle breaks every rule of prophecy and fantasy conventions. *The Sevenwaters Trilogy* and *The Bridei Chronicles* by Juliet Marillier are delightful fantasy series with an incredibly Celtic feel and much historical research…it all depends which aspects of *Game of Thrones* appeal the most.

Many other series are delightfully Tolkienesque though with mixed males and females and without the dull bits (heresy though it seems to say so). These include the following:

❖ Sara Douglass, *The Wayfarer Redemption*
❖ Guy Gavriel Kay, *The Fionavar Tapestry*
❖ Mercedes Lackey and James Mallory, *The Obsidian Trilogy*
❖ Patrick Rothfuss, *The Kingkiller Chronicles*
❖ Brandon Sanderson, *The Mistborn Trilogy*
❖ Tad Williams, *Memory, Sorrow, and Thorn*

Readers might also consider classic epics like *The Tain*, *The Mabinogion*, and *King Arthur*, all of which inspired parts of Martin's work.

What Are the Major Book and Show Differences?

Most shows take significant liberties with the books they're based on. Unusually, *Game of Thrones* changes almost nothing – scenes may be shortened, but often they're repeated word for word, especially the best lines. The websites that describe changes between the two are mostly stuck pointing out that Sansa meets Lady Olenna Tyrell in the gardens, not her chambers, and has a shorter scene in which she secretly confides her fear of Joffrey, rather than an hour-long one. A few scenes are added, but generally character moments that don't alter the plot. Characters' backstories, like Sam's rejection as his father threatens to hunt him in the woods, are also identical. A few specific differences involve character substitutions. Arya is supposed to be cupbearer to Roose Bolton (the Stark bannerman of uncertain loyalty) not Tywin Lannister. Jaime isn't captured and behanded by Bolton men but by the Brave Companions, a group of sellswords his father had hired, who then began running amok. Shae is the maid of a minor character who is not Sansa. There are many more Frey characters everywhere, wed to Lannisters and King's Landing characters as well as negotiating with Robb. Gendry inherits the plotline of the book's acknowledged Baratheon bastard, Edric Storm, as Melisandre seeks king's sons to burn. Stannis's wife and daughter (and the daughter's friend Patchface the fool) are seen often in the books, wandering about Dragonstone. Olenna seems to be negotiating in place of her pompous son. Sansa is proposed as a marriage candidate to Ser Loras's older brother, heir to Highgarden, not Loras. Each of these changes was made to simplify the overwhelming and confusing cast of characters, at least a bit. Family trees are trimmed, parts are combined, and so forth, but these differences are decidedly minor.

Many characters are introduced a book or two late, beginning their storylines only when necessary (Selyse and Shireen, Meera and Jojen, Thoros of Myr, and the Boltons fit this pattern). Thus minor characters and events shown, from Karstark's treason to Sam's finding a dragonglass horn on the Fist of the First Men will likely be needed farther along.

In probably the largest change, the show replaces Robb's sweet and passive bride Jeyne Westerling – whose father is a Lannister bannerman – with the capable and headstrong healer Talisa from Volantis. As she shows up, filthy and bloody, to tell Robb off for his lack of compassion, a far stronger character emerges. This change, as Martin has remarked at conferences, mainly was implemented as the television writers wanted to show Robb's romance (in the books his imprudent marriage appears as a complete surprise, with all the courting done offscreen). The meek little mouse was unlikely to gain anyone's respect or affection, so as new scenes of Talisa's character-shaping childhood with slaves were written, Martin suggested a new name for her new backstory.

And most brothel scenes are new, as is the character Ros. Martin comments:

> I like the fact that David (Benioff) and Dan (Weiss) are doing a faithful adaptation so when the scenes are the scenes from the books, I like those. And I like almost all of the new scenes, not from the books, that David and Dan and the other writers have added. The only thing that I miss is the scenes that are left out, scenes from the books that are not included in the TV show that I wish they would have included. As I watch a show I'm always thinking, "Oh, this is coming next" and then that scene isn't there. But I understand the necessity for that. We have ten hours and that's always we have. You cannot put every line of dialogue, every incident, in the TV show. You have to cut to the chase.[19]

Martin has been heavily involved, from casting decisions to writing a script each season ("The Pointy End," "Blackwater," "The Bear and the Maiden Fair"). He wrote many new *Twilight Zone* and *Beauty and the Beast* television episodes in the 1980s, and has even written some feature films. Of course, he's still busy writing the book series, with two more volumes to go (to say nothing of companion books, short stories, and other projects.) He adds:

> I talk constantly with David and Dan the executive producers and show runners. They've done an amazing job and stayed very faithful to the story. There've been some changes, but that's inevitable on a project like this. It's been a great ride so far and I hope it will continue for many years to come.[20]

The realism is reflected in the unusually large number of deaths in his series. Book fans note that no one is safe, and new watchers were shocked and angered by Ned's death after they'd grown to love him. Reactions ranged from amazement that a show would kill off the main character in season one to angry viewers canceling subscriptions. Martin has joked that he'll need to go into hiding at season three's end, when fans will be even more furious.

Despite the fan disagreements on the value of the plentiful sex and violence, the show is amazingly popular. Fans of the book are pleased with it, though there are occasional complaints of a beloved scene getting cut.

How Aged-up Are the Stark Children?

Martin notes:

> We had some real problems because Daenerys is only 13 in the books, and that's based on medieval history. They didn't have this concept of adolescence or the teenage years. You were a child or you were an adult. And the onset of sexual maturity meant you were an adult. So I reflected that in the books. But then when you go to film it you run into people going crazy about child pornography and there's actual laws about how you can't depict a 13 year old having sex even if you have an 18 year old acting the part – it's illegal in the United Kingdom. So we ended up with a 22 year old portraying an 18 year old, instead of an 18 year old portraying a 13 year old.[21]

Thus, as Martin explains above, everyone got "aged up." Events of the TV series are seventeen years after Robert's Rebellion, contrasted with the books' fourteen. Daenerys is 16 instead of 13. With her, the other characters are aged as well: Robb and Jon Snow are 17 instead of 14. Bran is 10 instead of 7 and Rickon's 6, not 3. Sansa is 13 instead of 11 and Arya is 11 instead of 9. Joffrey is 16 instead of 13, Myrcella is 12 instead of 8 and Tommen is 10 instead of 6. All this aging up is mostly for the nude scenes for characters like Daenerys and to fit a bit better with audience sensibilities.

These characters – especially those of the book – seem awfully young considering that Sansa's hand is being fought over, Jon and Robb are leading war parties, Arya's ranging the countryside alone and Daenerys is...well, doing everything imaginable. In fact, Martin had planned a five year gap in the middle of the series, which would have let them grow up a bit more,[22] but as it is, he'll likely have the book characters fulfill their plotlines younger than he had expected. He adds:

> The biggest thing I'm wresting with is the chronology. When I set out with the young characters it was my intention that the kids grow up during the series. And I thought I'd have a chapter. And the next chapter would be a month later. Then the next would be two months after that. And by the end of the book a year will have passed. But it doesn't make sense that a character will take two months to respond to something that happens. So you wind up writing the whole book and very little time has passed. After the third book I thought I would jump forward five years, then the kids would be older. That was part of the delay. I tried to write it with a gap but it just didn't work, so I wound up scrapping all that.[23]

Thus, though he wrote younger characters, the ones on the show are roughly the character ages he wanted. This is logical, as Daenerys, Jon, and Robb are now on the edge of adulthood, with Bran and Arya at the adolescent ages popular for adventuring fantasy characters.

How Feminist is Game of Thrones, Really?

Martin takes pride in his spectrum of female characters, from strong to sweet, saying:

> I wanted to present my female characters in great diversity, even in a society as sexist and patriarchal as the Seven Kingdoms of Westeros. Women would find different roles and different personalities, so women with different talents would find ways to work with it in a society according to who they are.[24]

Indeed, a *Salon* article notes:

> "Game of Thrones" persuasively demonstrates why some of us are always yammering on about the need for increased representation of women (and minorities) on television: Through the relatively simple process of upping the numbers, the burden on any individual woman magically lightens. No single character in "Game of Thrones" has to

be the show's final word on womanhood, and that's a freeing prospect. I can find Melisandre a dinner-theater-esque take on the sorceress archetype; you can find Daenerys an appalling victim of untreated Stockholm syndrome. But it's OK. With the women of "Game of Thrones," you don't have to put all your dragon eggs in one basket.[25]

Certainly, medieval women had few options, and Martin's women take full advantage of their world as warriors, healers, mothers, and more. Too many, however, ask men to take advantage of their sexual abilities, even those with career choices outside the brothels. Some see the stripping Red Priestess as feminist, others an offensive parody. *The New York Post* actually describes Melisandre, with "some mysterious witchy power in the amulet she wears around her neck. She's also got it in other places, as we saw in one graphic scene where she gives birth to a murderous shadowy wraith" as teaching viewers the following helpful message:

> Have a shadow demon in your loins and no one will mess with you. Less specifically: Develop a special skill that only you can offer, it will make you invaluable – whether getting ahead at your office job, or seizing the Iron Throne.[26]

Offer your boss sex and an illegitimate monster-child to get ahead in the office? To say nothing of creepy sex magic that kills people? Under the humor, it's clear Melisandre cannot be taken seriously.

Fans' views on the story's women vary, though like Martin, everyone seems to love Arya. Sansa and Catelyn have many supportive fans and many enemies calling them the weakest characters on the show. Cersei's fans are likewise mixed. The author of the blog Feminists-at-Large writes:

> Whether it is having her brother father her children to protect the Lannister bloodline or seducing key informants and strategic assets, Cersei firmly believes (as she tells young Sansa Stark) that "a woman's weapon is between her legs." She regularly defies the commands of her father, her husband the king, and all of the men on the Small

Council. The lioness of Lannister embodies feminism – even though she is a villain, through and through – because despite her life of luxury and privilege, she is not afraid to get her hands dirty to achieve her goals, nor does she allow any man to dictate her actions.[27]

This paragraph seems problematic – Cersei's feminist because she believes women should get what they want through sex? As Daenerys puts it, "The Copper King offers me a single ship on the condition that I lie with him for a night. Does he think I will whore myself for a boat?" (2.6). Really strong women have sex because they wish to, but not because they think offering men their bodies will give them power. It doesn't even work. Certainly, Robert and even Jaime grow to despise Cersei. Her offering or withholding sex doesn't affect them, they merely walk out in disgust. When Cersei literally tries sleeping with men to ensure their loyalty, beginning with her cousin Lancel in the second season, she loses at her game.

When Cersei suggests that she would make a better advisor than either of her brothers, Tywin dismisses her. "I don't distrust you because you're a woman. I distrust you because you're not as smart as you think you are. You've allowed that boy [Joffrey] to ride roughshod over you and everyone else in this city" (3.4). Her motherly love, like her "weapon between her legs" puts her family and realm in danger: When Cersei pulls Joffrey off the wall in "Blackwater," half the goldcloaks desert.

On a more objective note, if we apply the Bechdel Test, this series is in trouble. The test (named for comic strip creator Alison Bechdel) insists that a story must meet the following criteria:

1. It includes at least two women
2. who have at least one conversation
3. about something other than a man or men

Phrased in such cut and dry terms, it's hard to think of any in the show. Even Brienne's plea to fight for Catelyn is a result of King Renly's death. Sisters Arya and Sansa fight about Joffrey while sisters Catelyn and Lysa fight about Tyrion and little Robin. The book series likely has a few Bechdel-qualifying scenes in that many thousand pages, but offhand, only the sex scene between Daenerys and her handmaid comes to mind (yes, really). And even then, she's thinking of Drogo.

Too many strong women spend every appearance in show and book relating to, seducing, and otherwise completely consumed with obsession for men. Ygritte's every scene is teasing Jon Snow, Sansa's every scene is pacifying Joffrey or worrying about male characters' plans for her. A strong young woman like Meera Reed who spends all her time fussing over Bran and her brother or furthering *their* quest is discarding her own agenda to care for her world's dominant gender.

Further, the extensive nudity on the show is in fact sexist – female characters spend too much time stripping to manipulate the male characters and encourage their gaze. (Gaze is a concept in analyzing visual media—the male directors or cameramen often focus on female body parts, thus encouraging viewers to identify with male characters observing them, while treating female characters as objects.) In a now-famous Saturday Night Live sketch that emphasizes this problem, *Game of Thrones'* creative consultant is revealed to be a thirteen-year-old boy eager to see more. Admittedly, after season one, the amount of naked women contributing nothing but "sexposition" appears to decrease. But only after the show has established itself.

The strongest female characters with the most agency – Brienne, Arya, Yara, Meera Reed, Lady Olenna, and Catelyn – keep their clothes on at all times. (Brienne amends this in the bathtub scene of season three, but she and Jaime make it quite clear to each other that this isn't that kind of moment. And unlike every other nude female, she isn't taking off her clothes to please the opposite sex or the cameramen, any more than Jaime is.) However, Catelyn and Brienne, like Meera, Ygritte, and other strong women, spend all their time in service to the males in their life, as counselors, cheerleaders, and nurturers.

Lady Olenna and Yara are wonderfully strong females playing the Game of Thrones in their own right, but compared to Stannis, Robert, Renly, Littlefinger, Varys, Joffrey, Robb, Tywin, Viserys, Theon, Illyrio Mopatis, Mance Rayder, Balon Greyjoy, and Mace Tyrell (who like those two women are playing the game and do not take their clothes off to get power) they're notably a minority, with limited story arcs. If sex is how most female leaders like Cersei, Melisandre, and Margaery gain power, it's no wonder that Arya rejects the entire system.

Further, Brienne, Yara, Meera, and Arya completely reject their femininity – all are determined to be men in a man's world, from featureless clothing to strength on the battlefield. In one episode, Arya even dismissively comments that "most girls are stupid" (2.7). This hardly marks her as the height of feminist power. Women who loathe being women and spend all their time convincing others they're not just as good as (or better than!) men, they basically *are* men, are strong. But they make problematic feminist icons.

Besides Lady Olenna (who only has two scenes in the five existing books but fares better on the show), Daenerys seems the only strong, independent female enjoying being female, independent, and strong. However, she begins the show as the exploited rape victim who disturbingly grows to love her rapist and requests sex lessons so she can properly please him. (The book has a shy but curious Daenerys saying "yes" when Drogo asks on their wedding night and avoids this disturbing twist.)

Admittedly, from there, she grows into a liberated khaleesi and conqueror who (mostly) keeps her clothes on, but those first few episodes have done damage. Her triumphs are empowering and wonderful, but occasionally problematic. "Here I am – are you afraid of a little girl?" Daenerys shouts in the House of the Undying before she toasts the sorcerer with dragonfire (2.10). Her favorite phrase in the later books is "I am only a young girl and know nothing of war, but…" Granted, in medieval times, women often pacified and disarmed the patriarchy with such comments, but the khaleesi is establishing herself as a conqueror with an army. Jon Snow, roughly the same age and even less experienced at leading, would never shout, "I'm just a little boy, come and get me!"

Of course, there are great moments of power and agency: Sansa leads the women in prayer during the Battle of Blackwater. Shae beats Tyrion in a drinking game, revealing that she's nothing like he expected. Catelyn calls on an inn of her father's bannermen and kidnaps Tyrion. Arya's every moment sparkles.

But where is the girl who likes being female and takes power for herself rather than devoting every moment to a son or lover? Only in Daenerys, the formerly naked and exploited rape victim or Lady Olenna, whose story arc is limited. An even more severe problem is the many many weak women like Cersei and Shae who believe sex is the only path to power – a disturbing message for male and female fans both.

REFERENCES AND HOMAGES

Rome and the Ancient World

Rome has major correspondences, particularly in Old Valyria, the vanished empire with only roads, ruins, and fragments of lost technology remaining. Its former colonies speak a variant of its language, but much of its culture is gone forever. Since it vanished in a massive explosion, parallels with Atlantis out of classical myth appear. A few other story events particularly reference those from Rome.

- The Roman politician Crassus, a co-ruler with Caesar and Pompey, dies similarly to Viserys. He fought the Parthian Empire's enormous cavalry in the lands that had once been Persia. When he lost and was captured, the Parthians acknowledged his status as the richest man of Rome by pouring molten gold down his throat.

- Tyrion thinks, "His brother never untied a knot when he could slash it in two with his sword" (I:415). This references Alexander the Great who slashed through the ancient puzzle of the Gordian knot rather than meticulously working it out.

● The Titan of Braavos, a statue straddling the harbor, is a nod to the Colossus of Rhodes.

● The Spartans echo the Unsullied. In particular, the 300 Spartans at Thermopylae and the 3000 Unsullied at Qoroth.

● Arya thinks:

> "Maester Luwin had taught them about Braavos, but Arya had forgotten much of what he'd said... The city has no walls. But when she said as much to Denyo, he laughed at her. "Our walls are made of wood and painted purple," he told her. "Our galleys are our walls. We need no other.""

In the Persian wars, there was a prophecy about the "wooden walls" of Athens protecting the city. The general Themistocles decided this meant a fleet of ships and his navy defeated the Persians during the Battle of Thermopylae.

● Wildfire of course is the mysterious and corrosive Greek fire out of history. In the Siege of Constantinople, Emperor Leo III created an immense wooden barrier chain across the Golden Horn as it was called. Combining it with Greek fire created a devastating war weapon: Of the 200,000 troops who laid siege to Constantinople in 717, only 30,000 returned to Syria.

● Catelyn thinks, "For good or ill, her son had thrown the dice" when they cross the bridge at the Twins and commit to war. This echoes Caesar's famous "The die is cast" when he crossed the Rubicon and began his own civil war.

Medieval Europe

Martin comments:

> In 1981, on my first trip outside the United States, I visited England to see my old friend and writer Lisa Tuttle. I spent a month there and we went through the country visiting the most important sites. And when we were to Scotland we visited Hadrian's Wall. I remember it was the end of the day, near sunset. The tour buses were leaving and we had the wall nearly for ourselves. It was fall and the wind was blowing. When we arrive on the top, I tried to imagine how would be the life of a roman legionary of the first or second century after Christ. That wall was the edge of the known world, and it was protecting the cities from the enemies behind the wall. I experienced a lot of feelings there, looking to the North, and I just used it when I started to write Game of Thrones. However, fantasy needs an active imagination. I couldn't just describe Hadrian's Wall. It is pretty amazing but it's about ten feet tall and it's made of stone and mud. Fantasy requires more magnificent structures so I exaggerated the attributes of Hadrian's Wall.[28]

Hadrian's Wall inspired the Wall protecting the North from the "wildlings" or Scots. But many other correspondences appear as well. The "First Men," like the Celts, lived in harmony with nature and worshipped the trees and the Old Gods. The Saxons, after conquering the Celts, created their own "Seven Kingdoms": Kent, Sussex, Essex, Wessex, Mercia, Northumberland, and East Anglia. They echo the Andals of Westeros – the Saxons even originate from the same Germanic area as the Angles and Vandals. In this scenario, the most recent invaders are the Targaryens or Normans, the successful conquerors of the continent. Martin notes that Aegon the Conqueror derives from William the Conqueror, the Norman leader who made himself king of England.[29]

The land is England, warm in the south and icy in the North. Ancient ruins dot the landscape, reminding readers of ancient battles: Nightfort, Oldstones, and Summerhall carry the weight of history in a way not seen in America. Martin comments:

> The medieval setting has been the traditional background for epic fantasy, even before Tolkien, and there are good reasons for that tradition. The sword has a romance to it that pistols and cannon lack, a powerful symbolic value that touches us on some primal level. Also, the contrasts so apparent in the Middle Ages are very striking – the ideal of chivalry existed cheek by jowl with the awful brutality of war, great castles loomed over miserable hovels, serfs and princes rode the same roads, and the colorful pageantry of tournaments rose out of a brown and grey world of dung, dirt, and plague. The dramatic possibilities are so rich. Besides, I like the heraldry.[30]

Queen Isabelle of France and Cersei

Queen Isabelle of France, wife of Edward II king of England, was surprisingly aggressive for her era – she most likely had her husband murdered (much as Circe does) and campaigned to become regent for her young son, her lover ever at her side. On one occasion, she visited her birth family and, struck by the behavior of her two brothers' wives, accused both of committing adultery with various knights at the court. (The accusation may have been genuine, or she may have been attempting to move her young son ahead in the succession by eliminating rivals.) In 1314, Margerite de Bourgogne, wife of the future King Louis X of France, and her cousin, Blanche de Bourgogne, were put on trial.

The two knights were sentenced to be horribly killed, while the women had their heads shaved, and were displayed to the crowd and humiliated in the streets, and then were locked in the dungeons. After seven years of religious wrangling, Blanche de Bourgogne had her marriage annulled and was sent to a convent. Marguerite de Bourgogne died in prison, though there were rumors she was secretly strangled to facilitate the king's new marriage. Meanwhile, Queen Isabelle lost much popular support for starting the *Tour de Nesle* affair as the accusation and trial were named (*Tour de Nesle* was an old guard tower where the couples allegedly met). Readers of the fourth and fifth book may notice parallels.

Catherine de Medici and Cersei
Catherine de Medici, queen consort of King Henry II of France from 1547 until 1559, also has interesting ties to Cersei. At the age of fourteen, she wed, though the king excluded Catherine from participating in state affairs in favor of his celebrated mistress, Diane de Poitiers. When he died, Catherine found herself playing politics on behalf of her fifteen-year-old son, King Francois II, and then became regent for her ten-year-old son after the first's death. Upon *his* early death, she counseled her third son at statecraft as well.

Civil war was common at the time, and Catherine acted ruthlessly to keep her family on the throne at all costs. In particular, she and the uncles of Francois's wife, Mary Queen of Scots, battled heavily for power, much as Cersei does with the Tyrells. She made broad concessions to the Huguenots, religious rebels of the time. However, she didn't bother to learn the complexities of their position, and later found herself taking an angry hardline policy against them. Her attitude led to her being blamed for her sons' viciousness against them. However, her acts did indeed keep her three sons on the throne. She played the political game badly at times, but all she did was for her three children.

Like Cersei, her life was driven by prophecy – the famed Nostradamus told Catherine her husband would be killed in a joust, and her three sons would each take the throne after the death of the previous. As a child, Cersei received a prophecy from a Maegi called Maggy the Frog, much of which has already come true:

> Cersei: "When will I wed the prince?"
> Maggy: "Never. You will wed the king."

Young Cersei asks about Prince Rhaegar; she in fact weds King Robert instead.

> Cersei: "I will be queen, though?"

> Maggy: "Aye. Queen you shall be... until there comes
> another, younger and more beautiful, to cast you down and
> take all that you hold dear."

This younger queen might be Sansa, Margaery, or Daenerys.
Cersei exhibits paranoia and extreme jealousy toward Margaery
in particular, though she's a disturbing mix of cruel and warm
toward Sansa, her protégé.

> Cersei: "Will the king and I have children?"
> Maggy: "Oh, aye. Six-and-ten for him, and three for
> you....Gold shall be their crowns and gold their shrouds.
> And when your tears have drowned you, the valonqar shall
> wrap his hands about your pale white throat and choke the
> life from you." (IV:540-541)

This suggests all three children will be crowned, and also
predecease Cersei. If Joffrey, then Tommen, then Myrcella die,
all three will be crowned in the current order of Westeros
succession, though Myrcella will need a consort. In Dorne,
Myrcella would inherit before Tommen. This may be significant,
as Myrcella has been sent there and can be used for a puppet
queen in a civil war.

The word *valonqar* means "younger brother." Though Cersei
hates Tyrion, she gradually neglects, ignores, and dismisses
Jaime as a matter of course. It would be fitting if he turns on her
and they leave the world at the same time: "We will die together
as we were born together," as Jaime thinks (III:418).

Other Historic Parallels
- Two famous hunchbacks, Pepin, son of Charlemagne,
  and Richard III (according to Shakespeare at least), were
  both condemned by history and their families for
  plotting to take the throne and betray their more
  beloved siblings. Tyrion echoes them in many ways.

- A particular treacherous massacre in the third book
  echoes the famous "Black Dinner" in Scotland, as
  Martin has confirmed. Soldiers staying at Glencoe

massacred those who welcomed them as guests. The English king in the south arranged much of this and sent pardons to the wrongdoers, who were actually loyal to him. The idea of hospitality ran so deep at the time that this crime was considered unspeakably treacherous.

● William the Conqueror's funeral was disrupted by the horrible smell of the corpse…a particular book three funeral is equally nasty for the same reason.

● Charles Martel, grandfather of Charlemagne, reunited the Franks and halted the moors from entering his territory from Spain in the Battle of Tours of 732. Martin's Martells rule Dorne, a region based on southern Spain with much of its culture.

● Baelor Breakspear in "The Hedge Knight" and his unexpected tragedy resemble the fate of Edward the Black Prince

● The big castle in Edinburgh is on Castle Rock, like Casterly Rock, though there are others in the world.

● The civil war called the Dance of the Dragons (far back in Targaryen history) mirrors Empress Mathilda's struggle to inherit her father's throne while much of England preferred her male cousin Stephen. Upon winning, Mathilda was not allowed the crown in her own right, but had to settle for passing it to her son. The Dance of the Dragons confirmed that only males could inherit the Iron Throne. Daenerys may be in for trouble…

The War of the Roses

While other parallels appear, the War of the Five Kings appears to be a retelling of the English Wars of the Roses (1455-85), between the Houses of Lancaster and York like the Houses of Lannister and Stark. Many first names, only altered slightly, are shared between series: Jon, Robert, Edmund, Edward/Eddard, Richard/Rickard, Geoffrey/Joffrey, Thomas/Tommen, Walter/Walder, James/Jaime, Jane/Jeyne, Margret/Margaery, Marcella/Myrcella, Caitlyn/Catelyn, and Lisa/Lysa.

Henry VI of House Lancaster was placid and amiable when not seized by debilitating fits. His more forceful wife, Margaret of Anjou, claimed the regency and ruled through her young son, unfortunately cultivating his cruelty and violence. Cersei Lannister and her two sons are a close parallel, of course.

Richard Plantagenet, Duke of York and next in line for the crown, declared her son illegitimate and marched on London. Outnumbered, he was arrested and, like Ned Stark, forced to swear allegiance to the king. However, he later had a more successful bid, as he became "Protector of the Realm" and regent, as Ned Stark was meant to be for young King Joffrey. The Duke of York was even named King Henry's heir as a compromise.

However, Margaret refused to let her son's rights be put aside. Civil war began, north against south. The Lancastrians surprised and killed York, and stuck his head on a pike, but York's heir, Edward, defeated the Lancasters and was crowned King Edward IV. Margaret's son Edward died in a heroic last stand like Prince Rhaegar's. Henry VI was quietly executed in the Tower of London, and Margaret fled.

The new King Edward IV was fat and over-devoted to pleasure and women, much like King Robert Baratheon, who's based on him, as Martin acknowledges.[31] Despite negotiations abroad, Edward secretly wed Elizabeth Woodville, a politically unwise choice that angered some nobles as much as Robb's wedding. When Edward died suddenly from unhealthy living, illness, or possibly even poison, his youngest brother, the future Richard III, cut Edward's sons from the succession, claiming they were bastards. He also arranged for the death of his third brother, and many nobles he accused of treason. In this and other ways, he came to echo Stannis, the largely-disliked heir to his kingly brother.

At last, Henry VII, the last distant descendant of the

Lancasters, sailed from over the sea to defeat Richard and claim the crown (this plot will likely fall to Daenerys, the "prince who was promised"). Henry wed Edward IV's eldest daughter, Elizabeth, and united the red and white roses of their house sigils to create the Tudor Rose.

Cersei as Margaret and Robert as Edward IV are close analogies. Likewise, the realm in chaos at King Robert's death, with his children declared bastards and Starks and Lannisters vying for the throne echoes this time period.

How will this all end? It's unclear. Richard, Duke of York (basically the Ned Stark character) never inherited England, but his sons Edward IV and Richard III did, followed by Edward's daughter Elizabeth. Will Ned's son Jon Snow inherit such a destiny, ending the war by wedding the Targaryen heir, Daenerys? Or will Sansa make the dynastic wedding? Martin notes, "The Lancasters and Yorks fought themselves to extinction until the Tudors came in. But the Tudors were really a new dynasty; they weren't Lancasters. So..."[32] It seems the Targaryens will take the throne from both, after a fight nearly "to extinction."

Of course, Martin notes that his characters are only loosely historical:

> You can do one-for-one conversions of the real-world to fantasy, but if you're going to do one-for-one, you might as well just write straight historical fiction. Why write about a character who's exactly like Henry VIII? If you want to do that, then just write about Henry VIII.
> It makes more sense to take certain interesting elements of Henry VIII and certain interesting elements of Edward IV, and maybe something from here and something from there, and put them together and use your imagination to create your own character – someone who is uniquely himself and not exactly like someone from history. The same is true of the battles and things like that.[33]

The Lord of the Rings

Martin adds, "There are a number of homages to LOTR in my book. I am a huge Tolkien fan."[34] He comments:

> Although I differ from Tolkien in important ways, I'm second to no one in my respect for him. If you look at Lord of the Rings, it begins with a tight focus and all the characters are together. Then by end of the first book the Fellowship splits up and they have different adventures. I did the same thing. Everybody is at Winterfell in the beginning except for Daenerys, then they split up into groups, and ultimately those split up too. The intent was to fan out, then curve and come back together. Finding the point where that turn begins has been one of the issues I've wrestled with.[35]

With the Celtic and Norse elements set in a culture much like medieval England, these series have many strong parallels. There are also more deliberate small homages. From the "R.R." in Martin's author name to his mythic multiple hero war epic, he's determined to imitate the best.

Sean Bean

From the first episode, *Lord of the Rings* Star Sean Bean is riding about with sword and armor like Boromir (and like Boromir, he dies at the end of the first book). Bean comments:

> I do happen to enjoy playing those kind of roles: Riding horses, wearing wigs, growing beards. I do have an affinity to that kind of role and I think the good thing about "Game of Thrones" is there is such scope for it. With "Lord of the Rings" there were admittedly three films and they were thoroughly researched and very well replicated on screen but with what George [R.R. Martin] has created, it's a very different world that goes on much longer and has more twists and tales.[36]

Sam

The most blatant link is Sam. As Jon the hero's fat unheroic friend, he's like Sam Gamgee, practical and smart while his friend has grave responsibilities. Samwell Tarly is Jon's tie to the everyday world, and like Sam Gamgee, he grows from a humble buffoon (or "fat hobbit") to a hero.

Ravens

The Hobbit features a wise old raven, and Bilbo sends it with a message to Bard, the only one to remember the ancient secrets of speaking to birds. It's this talent among others that marks Bard as descendent of kings. Likewise, young warriors and poets in Celtic myth were trained in bird lore – those who could understand ravens' speech and sometimes take bird form could receive warnings of the future. It gradually becomes clear that someone is sending Jon messages through Commander Mormont's raven, who gives warnings like "burn" for the wight's attack, and at odd moments calls Jon a "king." He may have the blood of a king or be destined for kingship.

Ned vs Boromir

Martin's fans humorously insisted he pit his heroes and magic against those in Tolkien: Who would win in a fight – Nazguls or White Walkers? Smaug or Drogon? After varying amounts of consideration (and laughter), Martin chose Ice over Glamdring and said Tyrion would beat Frodo. Smaug and the Nazguls would decimate the field. And in an inevitable comparison, he bet the warrior Boromir would beat Ned the lord.[37]

The Decline of Magic

Dragons have been lost to the world, the children of the wood have all but vanished. Giants, krakens, and unicorns are rumored to exist, but all dwell far from the world of men. Daenerys's dragons may have brought back the magic, or it may be its last gasp before the power fades forever.

Many of Martin's characters go around "citing examples of how the realm was once better off and has now declined," as Linda Antonsson and Elio M. Garcia, Jr. note in their essay on romanticism in the series. They add:

> As one example, the Night's Watch has fallen on hard times. Their numbers are depleted and their cause neglected by most of the great lords and kings, compared to the past when, as Yoren describes it in A Clash of Kings, "a man in black was feasted from Dorne to Winterfell, and

> even high lords called it an honor to shelter him under their roofs."[38]

In Tolkien's world, the elves have nearly vanished, along with ents, dragons, and other magical creatures from the beginning of days. At series end, the greatest of the elves travel west forever, bearing the last of the magic rings. Martin's world may likewise see an end to the wonder of its world.

Other connections:

● Tyrion describes most lore about dragons as "fodder for fools" including "talking dragons, dragons hoarding gold and gems," and dragons telling riddles, all of which are clear references to *The Hobbit* (V:767). Tyrion also notes that the eyes are where a dragon is vulnerable "not the underbelly as certain old tales would have it" (V:759).

● There are rumors the folk of Bear Island are like Tolkien's bear-man Beorn, the skin-changer.

● Marillion the Singer is an homage to the band Marillion, in turn a reference to *The Silmarillion*.

● Daenerys's husband is named Drogo, possibly after Frodo's father of the same name.

● A castle on the Wall is named Oakenshield, like Thorin's name from *The Hobbit*.

● Several characters like Theon mourn that they aren't in a fantasy tale where heroes save the day and everyone lives happily ever after.

● The elves (children of the forest) and dragons have nearly vanished and many ancient creatures are regarded only as legend. Wights are undead monsters.

- "I have crossed many mountains and many rivers, and trodden many plains, even into the far countries of Rhun and Harad where the stars are strange," Aragorn says, compared with a description of a "town on the Summer Isles, where men were black, women were wanton, and even the gods were strange."

- Doom came to Old Valyria and to Numenor. In both cases, a minor house of the ruling class had a premonition of doom and escaped to the new continent, of which they then became hereditary rulers. Both dooms are specific echoes of Atlantis as well.

- Tyrion escapes in a ship at one point by hiding in a barrel. The dwarves of *The Hobbit* do likewise, though without the ship.

- Arya in the third book thinks of "the day without a dawn," a phrase appearing in the great battle of the Pellenor fields.

- Hodor throws a stone down the well and Bran says, "You shouldn't have done that. You don't know what's down there. You might have hurt something, or...or woken something up" (III:763). Pippin does that same act in the mines of Moria and indeed wakes a dark evil.

Other Fantasy Series
Robert Jordan

Martin is a fan of Jordan's and has cited the cover blurb by Robert Jordan for the first book to have been influential in ensuring the series' early success with fantasy readers. In *A Clash of Kings* there is a Sir Jordayne of the Tor whose banner is a golden quill – Tor was Jordan's publisher. The lord of the House is Lord Trebor, whose name reverses to "Robert." According to the *Song of Ice and Fire Campaign Guide*, their motto is "Let it be written."

Considering Robert Jordan's real name is James Oliver Rigney Jr., the following gains especial significance when said by Theon Greyjoy's uncle: "Archmaester Rigney once wrote that history is a wheel, for the nature of man is fundamentally unchanging. What has happened before will perforce happen again, he said" (IV:165). The opening of each Robert Jordan book touches on this theme.

The Princess Bride
There's speculation that Rugen the undergaoler references the villain Count Rugen and his monstrous dungeon. Oberyn Martell's repeating, "You raped her. You murdered her. You killed her children" when fighting Gregor Clegane certainly echoes Inigo Montoya's repeated "Hello, my name is Inigo Montoya. You killed my father. Prepare to die!" from *The Princess Bride*.

Tad Williams's *Memory, Sorrow, and Thorn*
Lord Willum's sons, named Josua and Elyas, are always quarreling, as with the feuding brother princes Josua and Elias in Tad Williams's *Memory, Sorrow, and Thorn*. Martin has acclaimed this series as a major reason for why he went forward with his own fantasy saga. House Willum's arms show a skeletal dragon and three swords, nodding to Williams's *The Dragonbone Chair*, and the three titular blades of the trilogy. Both series even feature a dwarf riding a wolf (though Martin's performing dwarf on a dog is satirically meant).

H.P. Lovecraft
Arya passes the Cult of Starry Wisdom, from Lovecraft's "The Haunter of the Dark." The Ironborn's Drowned God echoes the creature Cthulhu from his most famous works, while the common Greyjoy name "Dagon" is a Philistine water god seen in Lovecraft's stories. The religious saying, "What is dead can never die," echoes Lovecraft's "That is not dead which can eternal lie" in *The Call of Cthulhu*. The eastern city Carcosa is likewise from Lovecraft.

Jack Vance
As Martin notes:

> Jack Vance is the greatest living SF writer, in my opinion,
> and one of the few who is also a master of Fantasy.
> His *The Dying Earth* (1950) was one of the seminal books
> in the history of modern fantasy, and I would rank him right
> up there with Tolkien, Dunsany, Leiber, and T.H. White as
> one of the fathers of the genre.[39]

The castle Wayfarer's Rest echoes Liane the Wayfarer in *The Dying Earth,* and the castle Atranta is named for the fantasy world in Vance's *Bad Ronald*. The arms of both branches of House Vance show dragons, like Vance's novel *The Dragon Masters*. Other references include the sons of Lord Norbert Vance (who, like Vance, is blind): Ronald the Bad, Kirth (from *The Demon Princes*), Hugo (for his Hugo awards), and Ellery (for the Ellery Queen mysteries he ghost-wrote). The children of his brother Lord Karyl Vance offer more references: Emphyria (referencing *Emphyrio*), Rhialta (referencing *Rhialto the Marvellous*), and Liane. Lann the Clever, ancestor of the Lannisters, likewise echoes Vance's Cugel the Clever.

Conan the Barbarian
While Robert Baratheon is mostly based out of history, some see a Conan connection. The series by *Robert* E. Howard features a great battle hero who is unhappy when he takes over from a mad king. Both hero-kings are tall and dark haired with blue eyes, and share a fondness for wenching, drinking and eating. Cimmeria, like the Stormlands, emphasizes "dark shadowy forests and gloomy skies." And Valusia and Valyria are both great civilizations lost beneath the sea.

The Chronicles of Amber
House Rogers of Amberly with nine unicorns as sigil references Roger Zelazny's Amber books, in which the nine princes all use the unicorn as their family symbol. "Lord of Light," R'hllor's title, is also Zelazny's most famous novel. The Faceless Men offer another reference, as "walking the pattern" is essential in

the Amber books: "...and there is the entrance to the Patternmaker's Maze. Only those who learn to walk it properly will ever find their way to wisdom, the priests of the Pattern say" (V:844).

Other Series

● Lord Titus Peake is a reference to Mervyn Peake's famed *Gormenghast* trilogy, starring Titus Groan. Their banner has three towers, suggesting the series' moldering castle. Castle Ghaston Grey may be a similar reference.

● House Wyl features a black adder on its arms. Martin is known to be a fan of BBC's *Blackadder*.

● Merrit o' Moontown from the Brotherhood Without Banners references fantasy writer A. Merritt and his novel *The Moon Pool*.

● Khal Drogo crowns Viserys with melted gold much the way Ayesha, She Who Must Be Obeyed from the H. Rider Haggard story "She," kills her enemies by placing a red-hot iron pot over their heads.

● Ser Alyn Garner's shield has three grey owls, a reference to Alan Garner's *The Owl Service*.

● Alaric of Eysen: This minstrel references Phyllis Eisenstein and her minstrel character Alaric. *A Game of Thrones* is dedicated to her, as Martin thanks her for making him "put the dragons in."

● The names "Beric Dondarrion" and "Qhorin Halfhand" suggest Stephen Donaldson's Beric Halfhand the Lord Fatherer. Kevan Lannister may reference Kevin Landwaster from Donaldson's popular *The Chronicles of Thomas Covenant*.

- In the book *Thuvia, Maid of Mars* by Edgar Rice Burroughs, the titular young lady is often called "Thuvia, Maid of Ptarth." She has an enormous pet lion, which may allude to Brienne, Maid of Tarth, and Jaime.

- Lord Horton Redfort of the Vale has four sons: Mychel Redfort and Creighton Redfort may be a Michael Crichton reference.

- House Cordwayner may reference science fiction writer Cordwainer Smith. *Hammer*hal, their ancient seat, makes a logical smith's home.

- Two of Brienne's mock suitors from her youth include Harry Sawyer and Robin Potter. Brienne beats them both, unhorsing Harry and then giving Robin *Potter* a nasty *scar on his head*. Perhaps Brienne doesn't care much for the *Harry Potter* books.

Classics

- In the fourth book, some mummers are performing The Lord of the Woeful Countenance, a nod to Cervantes' Don Quixote, the Knight of the Woeful Countenance (IV: 507).

- Cersei comments that for all she knows, Tyrion could be hiding in Baelor's Sept, swinging on the bell ropes to make that awful din. This sounds like Quasimodo, the deformed bell ringer in Victor Hugo's *The Hunchback of Notre Dame*.

- "You were made to be kissed, often and well," Jorah says to Daenerys versus "You should be kissed and often and by someone who knows how," as Rhett Butler says to Scarlet in *Gone with the Wind*.

- The "Queen of Love and Beauty," a mystery knight defeating the other combatants, an unexpected, unmarriageable romantic heroine, and other trappings of the Tournament at Harrenhal are historically based but most familiar to modern readers from Walter Scott's *Ivanhoe*.

- Beric Dondarrion, the renegade lord hiding in the woods and proclaiming loyalty to the one true king, while robbing knights on behalf of the commoners, has strong parallels with Robin Hood. He even has a fighting priest – Thoros of Myr – a minstrel, and a man with a colorful cloak (Lem Lemoncloak) fighting beside him.

- In an interview, Martin discussed why his saga is called *Ice and Fire*, saying that the Wall and the dragons were "the obvious thing but yes, there's more." He noted:

> People say I was influenced by Robert Ford's poem [clearly, Robert *Frost*'s poem is meant], and of course I was, I mean... Fire is love, fire is passion, fire is sexual ardor and all of these things. Ice is betrayal, ice is revenge, ice is… you know, that kind of cold inhumanity and all that stuff is being played out in the books.[40]

> Fire and Ice
> by Robert Frost, 1920

> Some say the world will end in fire,
> Some say in ice.
> From what I've tasted of desire
> I hold with those who favor fire.
> But if it had to perish twice,
> I think I know enough of hate
> To say that for destruction ice
> Is also great
> And would suffice.[41]

This suggests two kinds of apocalypse—fire is as destructive as ice. A balance must be reached between the fire of volcanoes and dragons that caused the Doom of Valyria and the perils of the endless winter.

● Jon's friends express their book five anger with him in a moment straight out of Shakespeare's *Julius Caesar*. Martin borrows quotes from the play as Dolorous Ed warns Jon of danger, telling him his friends "have a hungry look about them…" (V:517), similar to Caesar's comment, "Yond Cassius has a lean and hungry look/ He thinks too much; such men are dangerous" (I.ii.190-195).

In both stories, the hero receives dark omens and warnings, from "Beware the Ides of March" (I.ii.18) to Melisandre's vision that "daggers in the dark" are coming and Jon must keep Ghost nearby. Around Jon, his raven and wolf act agitated. In Caesar's story, the graves open and the dead pour out, echoing the White Walkers. Calpurnia, Caesar's wife, dreams that his husband's statue, "Which, like a fountain with an hundred spouts/ Did run pure blood; and many lusty Romans/ Came smiling, and did bathe their hands in it" (II.ii.77-79). Jon's dream may be just as interesting and prophetic:

> Jon was armored in black ice, but his blade burned red in his fist. As the dead men reached the top of the Wall he sent them down to die again. He slew a greybeard and a beardless boy, a giant, a gaunt man with filed teeth, a girl with thick red hair. Too late he recognized Ygritte. She was gone as quick as she'd appeared. (V:769)

● Other mashed-up Julius Caesar quotes abound in the fifth book, emphasizing this parallel between stories: "Cowards die many times before their deaths/ The valiant never taste of death but once" (II.ii.32-37). Jojen Reed in turn tells Bran: "A reader lives a thousand lives before he dies…The man who never reads lives only one" (V:452). Varys says, "Those who die heroic deaths are long remembered, thieves and drunks and cravens soon forgot" (V:311) compared with Marc Antony's funeral words: "The evil that men do lives after them; /The good is oft interred with their bones (III:ii:74-75).

Television, Comics, Football, and More

● When Catelyn drags Tyrion along to the Vale, "Lharys, Mohar, and Kurliket," Lord Bracken's men-at-arms, come along. Martin has revealed these are the Three Stooges, Larry, Moe, and Curly.

● Lord Tommen Costayne of Three Towers references Thomas B. Costain, a favorite historical fiction writer of Martin's. The arms are a black rose quartered with a silver chalice, for his books *The Black Rose* and *The Silver Chalice*.

● The knight Courteney Greenhill references Greenhill, the minaturist who produces toy knights from the legendary Courteney molds, which Martin collects.

● A sailor comments, "Hacking off some boy's stones with a butcher's cleaver and handing him a pointy hat don't make him Unsullied. That dragon queen's got the real item, the kind that don't break and run when you fart in their general direction" (V:325). This last comes from *Monty Python and the Holy Grail*.

● The array of brazen beast masks at the book five pits contains "lions and tigers and bears" from a certain film.

● In the fourth book, some hedge knights wear a blue beetle, a thunderbolt, and a green arrow. Here we find the DC Justice League: Blue Beetle, Green Arrow, and the Flash.

- House Grell, with a green arrow, may reference *Green Arrow* comic writer/artist Mike Grell.

- Triarch Belicho of Volantis is noted for his run of undefeated victories until he was torn limb-from-limb by giants, like Patriots coach Bill Belichick, who had a similar run of 2007 victories until defeated by Martin's beloved New York Giants.

- Ser Patrek of King's Mountain is slain by the giant Wun Wun. Patrek's sigil, a blue star on silver, echoes the Dallas Cowboys, while quarterback Phil Simms's player number was 11, one-one.

Martin's Other Works

- The Fever River echoes Martin's novel, *Fevre Dream*.

- In the first book's prologue, Will says, "My mother told me that dead men sing no songs," nodding to Martin's *Songs Dead Men Sing*.

- The Hugo Award winning "A Song for Lya" features characters Robb and Lyanna caught in a tragic love story. The main plot focuses on a religion that sacrifices its members, a bit reminiscent of the red priests.

- "The Way of Cross and Dragon" short story introduces the Order Militant of the Knights of Jesus Christ (echoed in book four's Order Militant) and adds that the Biblical Judas was a dragonrider who carried three baby dragons about in a basket.

- "Bitterblooms" from *Dreamsongs Vol. 1* has the names Erika Stormjones and Northstar (echoing Stormborn and Darkstar), while the heroine is Alynne. (Alayne Stone is a viewpoint character in book four.) Alynne battles the frozen north, inhabited by vampires, in a world that's "cold and black and dead" like the North and its wights.

● "Slide Show" is the tale of volcanoes and tidal waves, like the Doom that took Old Valyria. "The world was full of storm and steam and fire," the narrator says, echoing the prophecies of smoke and salt.[42] Their ship is called Starwind, pointing toward Asha's Black Wind.

● "Starlady," one of Martin's science fiction stories from the 1984 collection *Sandkings* features the character Hairy Hal. This person also appears as a Night's Watch soldier – perhaps he was exiled for his unsavory behavior.

● House Swyft of Cornfield displays a blue "bantam rooster" on yellow. Their words are "Awake! Awake!" In fact, Martin's publisher is Bantam with a rooster logo – swiftness and waking Martin up may feature in the relationship.

● *The Hedge Knight* comic offers shields for the comic collaborators at the end: Dabell, Miller, Totroll, Crowell. Martin himself, as Ser Raymund Richard, has a shield depicting his previous works *Windhaven, Armageddon Rag, Fevre Dream* and *Dying of the Light*.

● A ship captained by Lord Baelor Blacktyde sails the ship Nightflyer, after the novella by that name.

● In the book two prologue, Maester Cressen tells Melisandre, "Only children fear the dark," referencing Martin's story "Only Kids are Afraid of the Dark."

● Maris, the heroine of Martin's *Windhaven,* is echoed in the book five sellsword Pretty Maris. The book is about a girl who longs to be a flyer but is discriminated against, echoing Daenerys in some ways.

● Bakkalon, the Pale Child, is a death god that appears in Braavos and in Martin's short stories "And Seven Times Never Kill Man," "The Way of Cross and Dragon," etc.

● Martin's *Haviland Tuf* series from the 70's and 80's inspired many *Game of Thrones* names. The short stories, attached together as a novel, were rereleased from Bantam in January 2013 as *Tuf Voyaging.* Characters include:

> ❖ Jefri Lion (Joffrey of House Lannister)
> ❖ Jaime Kreen
> ❖ Rikken
> ❖ The planet Vale Areen (Vale of Arryn)
> ❖ Celise (Lady Selyse)
> ❖ "Ma Spider" (Varys the Spider)
> ❖ Cregor Blaxon (Gregor Clegane)

Mythology and Religion

Bible

● Aeron Damphair is chief priest of the Drowned God on the Iron Islands. Moses's brother Aaron was chief priest of the Israelites.

● Lot's wife looked back while fleeing the cursed city of Sodom, and she became a pillar of salt. "Val stood on the platform as still as if she had been carved of salt. She will not weep nor look away" (V:137).

● Jacob was born clutching the heel of Esau, whom he betrayed for his birthright and fought with all his life.

Jaime was born holding the heel of Cersei – a rough time may be coming for them.

- Stannis accuses Alestor Florent of trying to sell his birthright for a bowl of porridge, a reference to a similar scene between Jacob and Esau.

- The new seven-part gods who are different aspects of a single one are "similar to the concept of the Trinity in mainstream modern Christianity," one critic notes.[43] Martin has said the same in interviews.[44] Much like Christianity in our world, the faith is a strong part of Westeros, from trial by combat to casual expletives and sacred oaths. The Great Sept of Baelor echoes great cathedrals of Europe. The High Septon anoints the king, and his support is essential for the monarchy. He himself echoes the pope or archbishop, with crowns, rings, and vestments of his office. Below him are Septons, brothers and sisters, sparrows, and so forth, much like the ranks of the church. In the fourth book, the Faith's emerging power likely alludes to an era of religious warfare and violence ranging from the Crusades to the Inquisition.

- The world of public burnings, proselytizing and devotion to the "one true God" sounds Christian, but it is based more in Zoroastrian tradition: In ancient Persia, Ahura Mazda was the lord of light and wisdom, ever-battling his dark counterpart Angra Mainyu. Likewise, R'hllor's priests call him "the Heart of Fire, the God of Flame and Shadow," and pray he will save them from the Other and his darkness (II.20). The word "Maegi," source of the words "magic" and "magician," comes from the Zoroastrians: The Maegi (the wise men who attend Jesus' birth) were seers and mystics, and sometimes charlatans, echoing the red priests from Melisandre to Thoros of Myr.

King Arthur

- Much of the courtly love tradition, including trial by combat and the queen whose adultery brought down the realm, are made famous by King Arthur.

- The Tower of Joy where Rhaegar takes Lyanna echoes the Joyous Garde where Lancelot takes Guinevere. Lancel Lannister is appointed to be the queen's special knight, but he has an affair with her instead, like Lancelot.

- There's a tale that King Arthur's father Uthor took the name Pen-dragon, head of the dragon, after he saw a dragon-shaped comet in the sky.[45] A comet also heralds the start of Daenerys's queenship and the birth of her dragons.

- The mythical twins Ser Arryk and Ser Erryk who die on each other's swords echo the Arthurian legend of Sir Balin and Sir Balan.

- Joffrey kills all the bastards of the throne, fearing other claimants, as Arthur tries doing to Mordred.

- Many characters from medieval romance, including Siegfried and Brunhild or the Arthurian Tristan and Isolde, lay a sword between them when they share a bed. Nimble Dick says to Brienne, "You could lay your sword between us," when suggesting sharing a bed to save money. Jon, who's clearly read the same books, uses Ghost for that purpose to protect himself from Ygritte.

Greek Myth

- Cersei, whose name doesn't match most of the English names of the court, is very reminiscent of her namesake

Circe. Like the Greek demigoddess, she beguiles men into making fools of themselves, discarding them once they've served their purpose.

- Littlefinger offers Sansa half a pomegranate when she's under his protection. Of course, the god of death offered innocent Persephone the same – by accepting, she agreed to be death's bride…Sansa, however, declines because they're "messy."

- In a scene cut from the show's Battle of Blackwater, Ser Loras decides to wear his lover and king Renly's armor into battle to make Stannis's army fear Renly's ghost is coming for them. In the *Iliad*, Patrocles does much the same, donning the armor of his lover and king, Achilles, to frighten the enemy.

- Prince Rhaegar's carrying off Lyanna and beginning a massive war that brings down his own family echoes the Trojan War and Helen's kidnapping.

Norse Myth

- Odin trades an eye for wisdom as he hangs on the World Tree. Bloodraven, with one eye, who watches the world and sees everything, is the closest parallel. He even wanders the world, hooded and cloaked like Odin as the king's spymaster. Later, he too is bound into a weirwood tree, source of ancient wisdom in the world. Odin was known for the two ravens, Thought and Memory, that sat on his shoulders and advised him, as Bloodraven's birds do.

- The kraken, symbol of House Greyjoy, is often seen in Scandinavian myth. It is a giant squid that swallows entire ships. The Drowned God's feasts beneath the ocean also resemble the Norse Valhalla.

- Frey, a Norse god of fertility, may be the source of Lord Frey and his enormous family.

- Tyr, the Norse god of war, was a mighty swordsman, of course. However, his bravery led to his downfall. The Fenris wolf, which would cause the world's end, would only let the gods bind him if one placed a hand in its mouth. Tyr did so, and lost his hand as the price for saving the world from the wolf. Jaime, notably, loses a hand because Catelyn frees him in exchange for her wolf daughters. (At the same time, many characters from myth and fiction have lost a hand. Luke Skywalker is often referenced by fans.)

- Meanwhile, the god Höðr or Hodor, was known for not being terribly bright, though certainly big and strong. The trickster Loki set him up to slay the young and beautiful god Baldur. One hopes this won't happen to Bran.

- Ragnarok, the Apocalypse of Norse myth, will be an endless winter, much like the one coming. This section from the Norse Twilight of the Gods shares parallels with Martin's series, book six of which will be called *The Winds of Winter*. (italics added below)

> SNOW fell on the four quarters of the world; icy winds blew from every side; the sun and the moon were hidden by storms. It was the Fimbul Winter: no spring came and no summer; no autumn brought harvest or fruit, and winter grew into winter again.
>
> There was three years' winter. The first was called the *Winter of Winds*: storms blew and snows drove down and frosts were mighty. The children of men might hardly keep alive in that dread winter.
>
> The second winter was called the *Winter of the Sword*: those who were left alive amongst men robbed and slew for what was left to feed on; brother fell on brother and slew him, and over all the world there were mighty battles.
>
> And the third winter was called the *Winter of the Wolf*.[46]

- The Gjallarhorn ("Shrieking Horn") will be blown by the god Heimdall to summon his brethren to the last battle of the world. Until that time the horn is buried under Yggdrasil, the world tree. Horns with unknown but incredible powers also feature in Martin's series.

- Joffrey, like the hero Siegfried, is born of ill-fated siblings. Daenerys comes from a similar heritage.

- Siegfried's father wears a wolfskin that gives him animal powers. Likewise Siegfried eats a dragon's heart to gain its magic – other sagas include devouring a wolf's or bear's heart to gain its powers. Daenerys of course eats a horse heart. All this leads to different kinds of warg magic.

- Tolkien's barrow-wights are inspired by the Norse draugar, creatures like vampires that rise from the burial mounds to attack the living. Martin's wights are similar.

- There is a fabled Norse cauldron that restores the dead to life, or at least a shadowy kind of life, allowing them to battle once more. Beric Dondarrion is restored to a similar life though he describes fading more each time.

- Hill giants and frost giants both appear in Norse myth – the giants beyond the wall combine elements of both.

Celtic/Irish Myth

There's quite a lot here, from single name references to major plot arcs.

- House Morrigen of Crow's Nest in the Stormlands likely references the Irish goddess Morrigan, who transforms into a crow.

- Morrigan was also known to change into a wolf and battle heroes, much as the Stark children begin to do. Wolves were associated with the wild, wisdom, and transformation, important skills the Starks must gain. The Irish werewolf was of a sort like Martin's wargs, a benevolent human who would sleep while his mind went into an animal.

- Cuchulainn the Irish culture hero is the subject of the epic *The Tain*, much like Odysseus or King Arthur feature in their own sagas. Nicknamed The Hound of Ulster for his role in guarding the king's household, Cuchulainn may be an inspiration for Sandor Clegane, the Hound. In Celtic myth, hounds represent hunting, fighting, and death, along with protection and guardianship.[47] Cuchulainn is a handsome warrior, but known for his "warp spasm," a kind of battle frenzy that overtakes him and mars his features. He wears a cloak of raven feathers when preparing for war, strengthening the concept of ravens bearing dark omens and violence.[48]

- "The Voyage of Bran son of Febal" is an epic poem describing a hero, like Brandon the Builder, who built a ship and sailed all the way to fairyland.

- The name Bran means crow or raven among the Celts. Crows were associated with the gods and prophecy, and sometimes were said to carry men's souls. They were also omens of war and death but would speak the truth to those wise enough to listen.

- In Celtic legend, King Bran (Blessed Raven) gave his sister Branwen away in marriage. However, in her distress, "she reared a starling in the cover of the kneading-trough, taught it to speak, and told it how to find her brother; and then she wrote a letter describing her sorrows and bound it to the bird's wing, and it flew to the island and alighted on Bran's shoulder."[49] Messenger birds are just as vital to Martin's series. Bran is not seen trying to rescue his sisters, but Jon is at one point.

● In battle to retrieve Branwen, King Bran was wounded in the foot with a poisoned dart. He bade his men to cut off and carry his head, which, still living, spoke and gave valuable guidance to his people. In his name, ravens are kept guarding the Tower of London, even today. Bran Stark too is crippled and must be carried, but he becomes a force of great wisdom, slowly reaching out to influence those he cares for.

● Robert dies gored by a boar. The boar is often directly or indirectly involved in the death of the hero in the great myths and epics, from Culhwch and Olwen to Adonis. In Celtic tradition, the boar was associated with courage and strength as well as sovereignty and protection of the land. "The ancient Greeks associated the boar with winter, so its killing represented the slaying of winter by the solar power of spring."[50] By contrast, this boar kills the king, and with his death, summer changes to autumn, just as the kingdom deteriorates into war. The courage and strength has killed King Robert rather than allowing him to prevail.

Likewise, the warrior Diarmuid stole away Grainne, his lord Fionn MacCumhail's betrothed. When he and the lady finally returned, Fionn and Diarmuid went on a hunt and Diarmuid was wounded by a giant boar. Fionn knew he could heal Diarmuid by letting him drink water from his cupped hands, but several times he let it spill through his fingers and Diarmuid died. From the affair to the betrayal and death of a warrior, Robert's death has parallels.

HERO'S JOURNEY, HEROINE'S JOURNEY

Jon's Hero Journey

The hero's journey as defined by Joseph Campbell is the great epic pattern behind all the great tales, from King Arthur to Siegfried. It's also the pattern behind *The Lord of the Rings, Harry Potter,* and most epic fantasy. The hero, an orphan or unloved foster child, leaves his home to venture out into the wilderness, the Otherworld of magic and mystery. Mentored by the wise old Merlin or Gandalf, he receives a magic sword and does many heroic deeds. In the wild, he meets a magical woman and learns about the world beneath perception, that of emotion and sensitivity. Thus enlightened, the hero develops his own magic, reluctant though he is to leave the world of rationality. Finally, the hero descends into the darkest place of all to face his ultimate foe, the shadow that is all he has rejected in himself: Darth Vader, Voldemort, Mordred. By understanding and defeating this opponent, the hero grows from boy to man, understanding the buried side of his own nature.

More than any other character, perhaps, Jon embarks on the classic hero's journey.

First, he has a mysterious parentage and grows up with a callous foster family. Catelyn suffers his presence, but considers his very existence an insult and treats him accordingly. Jon is the bastard, seated below the family table when the king visits, cast out when his father leaves for King's Landing. He cannot inherit by law.

As such, he sets his sights on the Wall, like his Uncle Benjen, their talented First Ranger. Producer D.B. Weiss notes that the Wall is "a merit-based society, which mostly don't exist" in medieval times or in Westeros.[51] For the young man dreaming of heroism and distinguishing himself as more than the unwanted son, it's a powerful lure.

His birth is shrouded in mystery, and many fans believe he's the child of Lyanna Stark and Prince Rhaegar Targaryen. If Jon is a Targaryen, he shares Daenerys' ancient magic and her destiny: Rhaegar insisted that he must have three children, that "there must be one more," since "the dragon has three heads." He said of Aegon "He is the prince that was promised, and his is the song of ice and fire" (II: 701). He had planned for three children, a conquering hero and his two sister-wives like Aegon the Conqueror had. If Jon is his child, he is intended to be husband to Daenerys, the conqueror reborn.

Beginning the Adventure

A Game of Thrones begins with Jon finding the direwolf pups in the woods. His is the homely rejected one, the discolored runt that echoes himself, ignored beside his legitimate siblings. Whether or not he has the blood of the dragon, he has the blood of the wolf, and the direwolf bonds with him. Working with Ghost, Jon develops prophetic shapechanger dreams. He sees Bran with a third eye, and in his dream, the heart tree gives him one as well, even as he enters Ghost and hears his thoughts (II: 559-561).

The Quest

Jon departs home and travels to the edge of the world, the Wall that separates the lands of Westeros from the lands of magic and otherness. Martin notes that "It's the boundary of the kingdom of the North. Beyond that is the wild, is the haunted forest. is lands where no one rules."[52] His mentors on the trip include such contrasting voices as Benjen Stark and Tyrion Lannister. Once there, Jon trains and swears his oath before the Heart Tree, just on the magical side of the Wall. "Once they had entered the forest, they were in a different world," the book notes (I:520). Executive producer David Benioff explains, "There are many dangers that lurk beyond the wall: beasts, the wildlings that are essentially northern barbarians, but the most fearsome are the White Walkers."[53]

Jon steps into the realm of the Other to say his words, risking his life to go ranging beyond the safety of the Wall. Once he's spoken them, he is appointed steward to Commander Mormont, making him in a way the heir to the throne. By Mormont's side, he begins to truly learn.

The hero's traditional quest is defeating the dark lord of evil – Jon soon begins searching hopelessly for his lost uncle Benjen, certainly killed or taken by the Others. As such, he has a personal grudge with the forces of darkness, and the oath he swears binds him to fight them: "I am the sword in the darkness. I am the watcher on the walls. I am the fire that burns against the cold, the light that brings the dawn," he vows. (I:520)

There appears to be an actual dark lord, though he's still unseen: "Beyond the Wall, the enemy grows stronger, and should he win, the dawn will never come again," Melisandre worries. His face is "cold and black and too terrible for any man to gaze upon and live" (V:410). Bran stares into the Heart of Winter and sees the Other, probably the spirit that commands the wights. It's not certain if this force is completely evil like Sauron in *Lord of the Rings,* despite Melisandre's fears. The battle between fire and ice may be a quest for balance, not for good to conquer wickedness. Of course, the hero's journey is traditionally the quest to conquer the father-tyrant and bring about a new reign of peace and prosperity. .

Faced with such a foe, Jon needs allies. Sam, his best friend, is like *Lord of the Rings'* Sam Gamgee, practical and smart while his friend has grave responsibilities. Sam chooses to swear his oath before a Heart Tree rather than the Seven, taking his own steps into the Otherworld. Soon both boys are summoned to their first mission, ranging beyond the Wall as the second book ends. "It's ultimately...the kind of a place that can break people or make them stronger," executive producer D.B. Weiss notes.[54] Jon and Sam indeed find their courage alone in the wilderness. Martin, when asked if Jon's fate will mirror Frodo's, quips, "He's taller than Frodo," but both heroes are undoubtedly preparing for grave suffering and torment.[55]

Beyond the Wall, Jon finds a cache of obsidian weapons and a mysterious horn. He gives the horn to Sam, who is destined for a world of magic and lore as Jon is destined for battle. Jon makes weapons of the dragonglass, which come to be more useful than he knows. He encounters the Others, terrible frozen dead brought to life, who herald his greatest foe. He also meets a lesser shadow who prepares him for his ultimate encounter.

Meeting the Shadow, Meeting the Goddess

The shadow archetype, described by Jung's philosophy, is the characteristics of ourselves we most detest or reject, projected onto another person of the same gender, as "the shadow cast by the conscious mind of the individual contains the hidden, repressed, and unfavorable (or nefarious) aspects of the personality."[56] If the son is unlearned, righteous, young, and powerless, he must face the evil tyrant who's wise and experienced. (Daenerys for instance faces the cruel but wise sorceress Mirri Maz Duur.) The shadow may be the villain, but his realm is the unexplored world of magic, mystery, and dreams waiting below the conscious personality. To Jungian scholars, though the shadow has been buried in the underworld, it has much to offer the questor, positive and negative.

> Envy, lust, sensuality, deceit, and all known vices are the negative, "dark" aspect of the unconscious, which can manifest itself in two ways. In the positive sense, it appears

as a "spirit of nature," creatively animating Man, things, and the world...In the negative sense, the unconscious (that same spirit) manifests itself as a spirit of evil, as a drive to destroy.[57]

Thus Jon and Bran both encounter the shadow force of good – mysterious heart trees, ravens, wolf powers and prophecies, along with the force of evil – the Other and its wights. Their wolves, Ghost and Summer, are also echoes of Jon and Bran's shadow selves – when one boy longs to lash out, to flee, the wolf often acts on these buried impulses or offers warnings of unseen dangers. Just as both boys are the products of civilization and the world of law, the wolves are guides from the Otherworld, tutors in magic and sensitivity.

Mance Rayder is a shadow for Jon, though not the ultimate enemy he will face before the end. Mance betrayed his oath to the Night's Watch to become a great leader, as Jon considers doing after his father's death. He has beautiful wildling women, subjects, and respect, all Jon has ever dreamed of. He even travels through Westeros, visiting Winterfell and the world Jon has denied himself. He's charming, friendly and flexible with honor as Jon is not. And the life he offers is tempting. At Mance's side, Jon can have Ygritte, a safe home, and glory. He need only betray his own people.

Jon's encounter with Ygritte, his first relationship, is a metaphor for encountering the wildness of the wilderness, so far outside the Wall that represents civilization and Jon's carefully-cultivated boundaries. Ygritte's favorite line is, "You know nothing, Jon Snow," as she becomes his teacher, educating him in the code of the wildlings and the world of nature. She guides him into a hidden cave with a pool – the feminine womb of magic and mystery. Caves are places of initiation: one enters a boy and returns a man, literally in the case of the show. This journey helps Jon understand the wildlings in a way other rangers don't. He thinks to himself later, "*You know nothing, Jon Snow. He had learned though, and Ygritte had been his teacher*" (V:464).

Descent
At the climax of the hero's tale, he descends into death, surrendering his life and all he is. This represents leaving one stage of life behind and entering another, after giving up all his childish illusions and facing the stark reality of his deepest fears. Scaling the Wall (ironically, an ascent not a descent) in the third book falls into this category as he nearly falls and literally faces his own mortality. After, he fights in a real battle for the first time and discovers the leadership skills that will take him far.

This descent also appears at the end of *A Dance with Dragons,* when betrayal carries him to a particularly dark place, though Jon may have another, darker challenge in the future. Jon dreams he's "armored in black ice, but his blade burned red in his fist" (V:769). In the future, he may be undead, he may be wielding Lightbringer, but certainly, symbolism of ice and fire surround him. He's the first to kill a wight with fire, he finds the lost dragonglass. He is the greatest hope against the darkness.

To complete the hero's journey, he must face the deadly Other and grow into a great leader of men and guide for others. Some heroes make peace with the force of darkness and others eradicate it entirely, but either way, Jon will grow into a leader who understands the Westerosi, Wildings, and Others in a way none has for a thousand years. Maester Aemon's frequent advice to him, to kill the boy within himself and let the man be born, is a summation of his hero-quest.

Bran, the Last Hero
Joseph Campbell, in his interviews with Bill Moyers, identifies the quests of the protagonist:

> There are two types of deeds. One is the physical deed, in which the hero performs a courageous act in battle or saves a life. The other kind is the spiritual deed, in which the hero learns to experience the supernormal range of human spiritual life and then comes back with a message.[58]

The former is Jon's quest, the latter is Bran's. Here are their hero journeys contrasted.

Campbell's Hero's Journey	Jon Snow	Bran Stark
The World of Common Day	The Starks adopt the wolves	The Starks adopt the wolves
The Call To Adventure	Benjen Stark visits.	Bran falls.
Refusal of the Call	Jon flees the Wall to help Robb.	Bran drifts, unconscious.
Supernatural Aid	Commander Mormont makes him his aide and gives him LongClaw.	He dreams of the Three-Eyed Crow.
The Crossing of the First Threshold	Jon leaves the Wall to say his oath and to go ranging.	Bran wakes and learns how to live again. He loses his home.
The Road of Trials	Jon ventures out with Qhorin Halfhand and joins the wildlings.	Bran quests North with the Reeds.
The Meeting With the Goddess Woman as the Temptress	Ygritte	Bran has a crush on Meera Reed.
Atonement with the Father Apotheosis Facing the Shadow	Jon serves Mance Rayder.	Bran meets Coldhands and trains with the three-eyed crow.
The Belly of the Whale The Ultimate Boon	In book five, Jon begins his dark descent. Winter is nearly here.	*When only the Last Hero remained, the Others attacked...*
Refusal of the Return The Magic Flight Rescue From Without The Crossing of the Return Threshold	Jon will face conflicting temptations: Starks, wildlings, power, love, and the Wall.	Bran will face conflicting temptations: the physical and spiritual worlds.
Master of the Two Worlds Freedom To Live	Jon masters the magical world and also becomes a leader of men.	Bran balances magic with his loyalty to friends and family.

Bran crosses his first threshold when he sees the forbidden in the first episode and Jaime pushes him out the window. Thus, Bran has a short death-and rebirth sequence, lying unconscious for days and then waking a cripple. This is a transformation from childhood into adolescence, like that Sleeping Beauty undergoes. "During puberty, sleep is the refuge in which an adolescent girl can absorb the new sense of herself that she gains from the prick of the spindle, and changes from girl to woman," explains Gould.[59] Likewise, Bran is transforming from a younger son of Winterfell into a greenseer and warg, the prophet and magician who will save the world.

He has the ancient magic, as shown by the extraordinary perception of Summer: "When Summer defends Bran and Catelyn, divine powers seem to be intervening to protect the young Stark family."[60] The wolf's name suggests the magic of fire, needed to fight the Other and his frozen world, just as the wolf's presence awakens Bran's visions. In the realm of the unconscious, Bran has a powerful dream of what is to come, and thus his mentor tells him his destiny:

> He lifted his eyes and saw clear across the narrow sea, to the Free Cities and the green Dothraki sea and beyond, to Vaes Dothrak under its mountain, to the fabled lands of the Jade Sea, to Asshai by the Shadow, where dragons stirred beneath the sunrise.
> Finally he looked north. He saw the Wall shining like blue crystal, and his bastard brother Jon sleeping alone in a cold bed, his skin growing pale and hard as the memory of all warmth fled from him ... North and north and north he looked, to the curtain of light at the end of the world, and then beyond that curtain. He looked deep into the heart of winter, and then he cried out, afraid, and the heat of his tears burned his cheeks.
> Now you know, the crow whispered as it sat on his shoulder, now you know why you must live.
> "Why?" Bran said, not understanding, falling, falling.
> Because winter is coming. (I:136-137)

Bran accepts his destiny but nonetheless remains in the

castle, acting as the Stark of Winterfell while Robb is on campaign.

A second Call arrives in the form of Theon, who captures Winterfell. Bran escapes with Osha and the Reeds, forced to go out into the world. This is a sort of death-descent as well, as he hides in the crypts and leaves everyone to think him dead. As he travels, Jojen advises him of his destiny. Bran resolves to find the three-eyed crow who's been calling to him rather than seeking safety with Jon on the Wall.

He remains strangely insistent that no one know he's alive – twice he passes near Jon and refuses to alert him. It's clear that his mission is more important than taking his role as a Stark of Winterfell, more desperate than his need to see Jon. Further, the hero's journey, a quest of growth into adulthood, cannot be taken with a babysitter. "There are times in life where we must be unreachable, times when we must insist that those around us, especially those nearest and dearest, remain at a distance if anything significant is to develop inside us," explains Gould.[61] Thus Bran maintains his secrecy.

North beyond the Wall, Bran finds the three-eyed crow and trains with him. Bran learns to fly within the minds of crows and watch the past, present, and future through the eyes of heart trees. He encounters the mysterious children of the wood. During his training, he learns to reach out to Jon and Theon, to be the eyes that see across the world. Many heroes like Luke Skywalker become part of the magic and never truly return to their old lives. Even if Bran never leaves his hidden cave, he will play a part in the war to come.

In the book, Old Nan entertains Bran with a story about the White Walkers: Thousands of years ago, in a winter night that lasted a generation, the Others came, and they hated "iron and fire and the touch of the sun" (I:240). The last hero of the First Men set out to find the children of the forest, whose ancient magics could restore mankind's lost wisdom. He left with his sword, a dog, his horse and twelve companions. When only he was left, the Others attacked…and then the tale is interrupted.

When Bran and Rickon bid goodbye to Maester Luwin in the Godswood, there are six of them – exactly half of twelve, just as half of Bran is left to be a hero. This list includes Bran, Rickon, Hodor, Osha, Jojen, and Meera (in the book, these last two escaped with the Starks).

If one adds the guides, travelers and helpers the children find on the way North, one can make the count up to exactly twelve, though most are temporary. Bran has no horse, but he has a wolf of course. As he travels steadily north, his story mirrors the Last Hero's. The classic hero's journey always involves descending into the darkest place completely alone. Thus Bran will lose all his friends eventually and confront the Other, as he does in his book one dream.

There's an intriguing Celtic poem that echoes much of Bran's destiny. In Celtic myth, "Bran" means raven. Many heroes, including several Brans, journeyed into the land of the elves and fairies, under the burial mounds. Old Nan's children of the forest, whom she describes as "the first people, small as children, dark and beautiful" live underground (I.736-37). The poem describes the elves' search for a great hero:

> 53. He will be in the shape of every beast,
> Both on the azure sea and on land,
> He will be a dragon before hosts at the onset,
> He will be a wolf of every great forest.
> ...
> 58. He will be – his time will be short
> Fifty years in this world:
> A dragonstone from the sea will kill him
> In the fight at Senlabor.
>
> 59. He will ask a drink from Loch Ló,
> While he looks at the stream of blood,
> The white host will take him under a wheel of clouds
> To the gathering where there is no sorrow.[62]

The curious reference to a "dragonstone" (ultimately revealed to be a slingstone) and shapechanging suggests a connection between tales. Will Bran Stark bond with a dragon and soar into the skies? Will he vanish into the realm of the children and weirwoods? Or die young, sacrificing himself to save the world?

The Heroine's Journey

Though scholars often place heroine tales on Joseph Campbell's famous hero's journey chart point by point, the girl has always had a notably different journey than the boy. She quests to rescue her loved ones, not destroy the tyrant as Harry Potter or Luke Skywalker does. The heroine's friends augment her natural feminine insight with masculine rationality and order, while her lover is a shapeshifting monster of the magical world – a frog prince, beast-husband, or two-faced vampire. The epic heroine wields a magic charm or prophetic mirror, not a sword. And she destroys murderers and their undead servants as the champion of life. As she struggles against the patriarchy – the distant or unloving father – she grows into someone who creates her own destiny.

Eventually, she descends into the underworld there to die and be reborn greater than before. Awaiting her is the force of destruction itself, in this case, the evil Other bringing unending winter to the world. The heroine not only defeats this force, she grows from the lesson and rejoins the world as young mother, queen, and eternal goddess.

Heroic Gifts

Daenerys has magical Targaryen gifts, immune to fire and illness as she is (V:473). And she has a destiny: A child of the forest said that "the prince that was promised would be born of their line," the line of her parents Aerys and Rhaella (V:300-301). (Maester Aemon notes that the word "prince" is gender-neutral in the prophecy, reflecting the nature of dragons.)

At the same time, Daenerys receives a number of talismans, particularly during her wedding scene. She's given three fine weapons, which she uses to gain her bloodriders. Drogo brings her the magnificent silver horse. Ser Jorah gives her books of Westeros, land of her past and future. And Illyrio, who brokered the marriage, gives her the three dragon eggs.

"The universe begins with roundness; so say the myths. The great circle, the cosmic egg, the bubble, the spiral, the moon, the zero, the wheel of time, the infinite womb; such are the symbols that try to express a human sense of the wholeness of things," writes Barbara G. Walker in *The Woman's Dictionary of Symbols and Sacred Objects*.[63] Thus the egg and circle are divine symbols of the lifecycle. They represent the woman as life-giver and font of intuitive wisdom, allowing her to channel the future. Eggs are a popular feminine symbol, representing life and fertility, symbols of the heroine herself. Eggs also represent potential, important for the innocent and untried Daenerys who grows alongside them into a conqueror and queen. Eggs are the entire lifecycle bound in a single sphere, simple of reincarnation and rejuvenation. As such, they feature in Easter and Passover traditions, coinciding with a time of spring and rebirth. Several cultures traditionally eat eggs after a death. Chinese and Native American legend has the world beginning as a single egg, which opens to reveal everything inside. Daenerys's eggs are all these things for her, resurrecting her as a mother, guardian of not only three dragons but a world in which magic itself has been reborn along with her. The comet itself, round and red in the sky, might be seen as an egg of sorts.

While the hero always carries a magic sword, heroines get books and spyglasses, potions and amulets. This echoes a subtler form of questing, with cleverness, healing, and perception in place of combat. The books Ser Jorah gives Daenerys give her a clearer picture of Westeros than that her brother offers. They are tools of divine intuition, offering the heroine powers of wisdom and prophecy.

Her beautiful horse makes Daenerys believe her new husband has given her the wind, an image of freedom (as she comments in the book). With it, the young khaleesi is no longer a sheltered princess but a rider of the Dothraki. Silver is the color of moon magic and feminine strength like Artemis's bow or Galadriel's ring. Silver's mirrorlike clarity suggests vision and deep knowledge, while the metal itself is shapeable yet strong. The heroine's path mirrors this, blending flexibility and endurance.

Mentor

Daenerys has several mentors, including Ser Jorah and Barristan the Bold. However, her most significant mentor is the Maegi Mirri Maz Duur. The Dothraki describe her as a woman who "lay with demons and practiced the blackest of sorceries, a vile thing, evil and soulless, who came to men in the dark of night and sucked life and strength from their bodies" (I:671). The mentor of the heroine's journey is no kindly Gandalf or Merlin. Instead, she is the wicked stepmother of Snow White, choking the innocent maiden with tight corsets and a poisoned apple as she forces her to face the cruel reality of adulthood. The original Little Mermaid has the unfeeling sea witch, who cuts out her tongue, not cruelly, but as a fair price for her services. Even the mermaid's grandmother is callous to suffering, clipping sharp oysters to the girl's tail to indicate her rank. Many myths reflect this relationship:

> Venus's initiation of Psyche is demanding in the extreme. Psyche suffers torments and afflictions; she despairs of accomplishing her tasks and becomes suicidal. But these strenuous labors develop her consciousness and her capacity to love. The Terrible Mother is the heroine's catalyst. She represents the dark, unexplored side of the heroine, a side Psyche still must face.[64]

Daenerys's lot is much the same.

These are the typical mentors for the heroine, and the Maegi is no exception. While the show sees her using a poisoned dressing on the Khal, the book is more ambiguous – The Khal pulls off the dressing because it stings, and the wound festers. If he had followed directions, the Maegi insists, he would have survived. Harshness and pain are part of life, the mentor teaches.

Whether or not that's true, the cruel mentor's job is to force the innocent heroine to face the harsh realities and ugliness of her own mortality. "The gaps from housewife to career woman; from wife to widow; from widow to lover; from lover to single woman again: all involve pain and ungainliness and a change of consciousness," notes Joan Gould, author of the fairytale analysis *Spinning Straw into Gold*.[65]

Snow White's stepmother makes her eat the apple, the thirteenth fairy pricks Sleeping Beauty with a spindle. And the Maegi strikes her terrible bargain: a life for Drogo's. She teaches Daenerys the value of life and of making bargains without considering: When Daenerys protests that she would not have willingly sacrificed her child, the Maegi can only say that Daenerys secretly knew the true cost. The mentor's job is to make the heroine accept these grim realities, rather than ignoring them. A girl can live in innocence, but to be a mother, one must know the pain and ugliness of real life. As Silvia Brinton Perera comments in *Descent to the Goddess,* "Until the demonic powers of the dark goddess are claimed, there is not strength in the woman to grow from daughter to an adult who can stand against the force of patriarchy."[66]

Like Mance is for Jon, this dark mentor represents the shadow, all the protagonist isn't but must learn from to tap these skills within the self. Cersei tutors Sansa this way, showing her the grislier side of life as a woman. Daenerys indeed learns from the Maegi's betrayal: that kindness will not earn her kindness, that life is needed to buy life. It is a far harder, crueler Daenerys who burns the Maegi in the fire, for only this cruelty can allow Daenerys's dragons to be born.

More mentors come to Daenerys as the series progresses: After the dragons arrive, Quaithe appears to Daenerys and offers her perplexing riddles:

> "To go north, you must go south. To reach the west, you must go east. To go forward you must go back, and to touch the light you must pass beneath the shadow."
> Asshai, Daenerys thought. She would have me go to Asshai. "Will the Asshai'i give me an army?" she demanded. "Will there be gold for me in Asshai? Will there be ships? What is there in Asshai that I will not find in Qarth?"
> "Truth," said the woman in the mask. And bowing, she faded back into the crowd. (II.426)

On the show, the masked woman of Qarth is more direct, cautioning Ser Jorah that Daenerys faces danger: "I'm no one but she is the Mother of Dragons. She needs true protectors, now more than ever...They are dragons, fire made flesh. And fire is power" (2.5). Of course, it is possible this mentor will be another source of cruelty, torturing Daenerys when she travels southeast as ordered – what Daenerys needs will certainly not be what she would choose for herself, as her season one arc reveals.

Mirri Maz Duur is Daenerys' first magical mentor, Quaithe is the second. Melisandre may become the third.

Daenerys and Men

On the heroine's journey, the young woman is surrounded by males who evoke her untapped masculine side and teach her to use its power. This animus, or male archetype, "evokes masculine traits within her: logic, rationality, intellect. Her conscious side, aware of the world around her, grows, and she can rule and comprehend the exterior world."[67] This is Jungian analyst Marie Louise Von Franz's model, adapted into a chart for easy viewing.

The Animus Growth Within the Heroine	Trait	Positive Aspect	Negative Aspect
Passion and Physical Force	Emotion	Mutual devotion	Mutual rage and destruction
Initiative and Planning	Body	Useful plans and action	Harmful, ill-considered acts
Law, Rule, and Order	Mind	Self-restraint and moral advice	Inflexible obstruction
Wisdom and Spiritual Fulfillment	Spirit	Guide to self-knowledge and ascension	Deceiver and distorter of the future

Viserys certainly embodies passion and physical force as he manhandles and even gropes his sister, making ribald comments and demanding his birthright, the throne. He threatens to kill slaves, hits them and his sister, and even jeers at powerful warriors. He has inherited the family madness, invoking emotion without any self-control. His rage indeed leads to his own destruction, though Daenerys has the sense not to interfere.

If Viserys is childish untempered emotion, Khal Drogo is the body – force and physical splendor, energy and rule through strength. Their son, the Stallion Who Mounts the World and conqueror of nations, echoes him, as do his warriors. Whether they respect Daenerys or antagonize her, impulse, passion, and swordplay are their first resort. Under Drogo's influence and filled with love for him, Daenerys trusts the Maegi who offers dark magic to save Drogo, following her heart rather than her head. This intemperate act leads to Drogo's death as well as her son's.

Ser Jorah is the mind, always a figure of restraint and wise counsel rather than action. His practical advice remains bloodless and expedient rather than emotionally based as he counsels Daenerys to sell the dragon eggs, abandon her dying husband, and later leave the dragons behind in the House of the Undying. This is all the rational course to take, if one sets aside the deeper feminine wisdom born from dreams and love that's blossoming within Daenerys. She ignores his advice, like ignoring the rational voice within herself, and wins the day through the deeper wisdom of faith and love.

The second book introduces male villains: the Qartheen dignitary Xaro Xhoan Daxos, who is calculating and expedient like Jorah, and Pyat Pree of the Warlocks of Qarth, the evil spiritual guide, deceiver and distorter of the future. Xaro is always scheming and plotting with his rise to power and wealth. He offers Daenerys marriage in return for his aid to conquer the Seven Kingdoms. This is not for love, but for power and political gain. However, he betrays her when she refuses him, and he seizes control of the city through treachery. Having learned during her time in the magnificent patriarchal city, Daenerys outwits him, locking him in his own impenetrable vault on the show. By the second season's end, she's beginning to master the calculating world of the intellect.

Battling the Patriarchy, Battling Pity

As Daenerys travels, she outwits the arrogant slaver of Astapor by offering him her largest dragon in trade. Like the Starks' wolves, Daenerys's dragons reflect her buried feelings, all the wrath and power she's only beginning to integrate into the self. The slaver cannot control the dragon and is burned to ashes. By letting out her hidden strength in careful bursts, controlling and guiding it, Daenerys gains an army.

Ser Jorah points out that the Unsullied do not kill civilians or rape women, unlike other soldiers. Back in Westeros, Rhaegar's love or lust for Lyanna and Jaime's for Cersei have both begun civil wars. As the slaver of Astapor points out, the Westerosi men sworn to chastity soon break their vows. "Their days are a torment of temptation, any fool must see, and no doubt most succumb to their baser selves" (III:317). The Unsullied by contrast have been castrated of their emotional and physical urges to be a perfect fighting force, completely obedient to the will of Daenerys. As such, they symbolize a new kind of soldier in service to the reigning queen, bodies without destructive emotion.

The Unsullied are a fit army for the mother of the downtrodden: They worship a goddess they call the "Mother of Hosts," an echo of Daenerys herself. As former slaves, they are also victims Daenerys longs to free. Recruited as five-year-old children, robbed of even their names, castrated and forced to murder their own puppies, they have been brutalized, stripped of all individuality and self-worth. Two children are killed for every Unsullied who survives. Daenerys ends the brutal practice of making Unsullied. She also returns their names and with them the beginnings of their identity.

As the mother-protector of her growing community, Daenerys also frees the slaves and stays in the east to protect them. The slavers' symbol is the harpy, a female monster that would afflict the innocent, snatching their food and rending them with claws. By battling them, Daenerys sets herself as a hero-protector. However, in her campaign for Westeros, staying in the east is a disaster. To Slaver's Bay, she is no legendary Targaryen, only a barbarian conqueror determined to destroy their way of life. As terrorist attacks escalate, Daenerys refuses to respond in kind and forbids anyone to harm her underage hostages.

Male heroes are tested by having to endure pain, hunger, and thirst to prove their forbearance – the strength of self all heroes need to overcome their initiation. Heroines, however, must resist pity, withstanding the claim of what is nearby for the sake of a distant abstract goal. This is a task of single-mindedness, of willpower.

Daenerys is famous for protecting the weak, whether it is the Lamb Men in the first book or the mute slaughtered children of the third, all pointing voicelessly at the city Daenerys conquers in retribution. "Before long, she was actively inciting change in the hyper-masculine Dothraki culture – particularly when she appealed to her husband to stop the systematic rape of captured women," one critic notes.[68] However, intervening often makes things worse for people in the long run, as with the girl Eroeh.

Daenerys thus learns to resist pity, allowing her brother's execution even as he calls for her aid. Though tempted by Drogo and her child awaiting her in the House of the Undying, she leaves them behind. She takes pity on diseased people of Astapor, but won't allow them to endanger the people of Meereen. Daenerys even chains up her dragons when one does the unspeakable.

On many occasions, she punishes those who betray her and those too dangerous to live, though she tries to spare the innocent, sometimes to her regret. Martin adds, "Daenerys is still very young. She has lessons to learn. That [conquering a city and killing hundreds of slaveowners] was one of them. It is not as easy to do good as it might seem, no matter how noble your intentions."[69] A similar test may await her at the series' climax.

Death and Rebirth

The hero and heroine always descend into death only to be reborn more powerfully – as the Ironborn would say, "What is dead may never die, but rises again, harder and stronger." In fact, the Ironborn embody this journey, deliberately drowning themselves literally or symbolically to enter new stages of life. While this is a metaphor for undergoing trauma or despair and growing stronger from the challenge, fantasy tends to address this literally. Daenerys faces death in the first book when Drogo is fatally wounded: She loses her child, she enters the tent of death, she nearly dies herself, and she finally gains the wisdom and pitilessness to slay the shell that remains of Drogo. "If her treatment of the witch Mirri Maz Duur in last night's episode is any indication, Daenerys has no mercy left in her," one reviewer comments.[70]

Indeed, she lashes the Maegi to the fire and enters it herself, vanishing into the flames all night and burning down to her core – clothing, hair, all that concealed her is burned away, and a new Daenerys rises from the ashes, no longer the marriage pawn and subservient wife of Drogo, but a leader of men and the Mother of Dragons. On the threshold of death, she calls herself Daenerys Stormborn of House Targaryen for the first time— she's growing from khaleesi to conquering queen.

> Coming out of the fire naked, with her three young dragons, it was as if she'd been reborn. Though Daenerys loved Khal Drogo, she doesn't need him anymore; she can raise a khalasar on her own. If Daenerys is truly "the dragon," the hatched eggs are almost a surrogate for the son she lost in childbirth. And with her new allies, she's poised to take back the iron throne.[71]

The comet, an ancient symbol for dragons, blazes overhead.[72] The egg that was Daenerys has broken open at last.

As Melisandre the Red Priestess foretells:

> When the stars bleed and the cold winds blow, a warrior shall draw from the fire a burning sword. That sword will be Lightbringer. The one who draws it will be Azor

Ahai...When the red star bleeds and the darkness gathers, Azor Ahai shall be born again amidst smoke and salt to wake dragons out of stone.

Dragonstone, Daenerys's birthplace, is covered in volcanoes and surrounded by sea. Amidst tears and a funeral pyre, Daenerys is reborn under the red comet as a figure of prophecy and magic, dragons woken from their petrified eggs.

The first book of a series often covers the entire mythic journey, as does the series as a whole, serving to entice readers early and keep them present for the entire epic. *Star Wars* and *Harry Potter,* among others, follow this pattern. Thus, while Daenerys dies and is reborn in the first book, this almost certainly echoes a more dramatic death and rebirth at series' climax.

In fact, just as the first book revealed her dazzling destiny and hidden powers, another revelation may appear in the final book. Through their Targaryen bloodline, Rhaegar and Daenerys have prophetic dreams like the Starks. Also like the Starks, Daenerys raises her special pets, sigils of her house, from babies so that they trust and defend only her. It's possible that the Targaryens, like the Starks, have the power of animal transformation and Daenerys will ride in the mind of her dragons, as Bran does with Summer. Her ancestor Brynden "Bloodraven" Rivers is a warg with no Stark or Northern blood at all.

Aerion the Monstrous dreamed he could transform into a dragon so he drank wildfire and died, while Mad King Aerys believed if he burned his city with wildfire he would rise from the ashes, a dragon. His son prince Viserys, like his ancestor Prince Aerion from "The Hedge Knight," threatens that Daenerys will "wake the dragon." All four claim that they *are* the dragon—it seems likely their prophetic dreams are feeding their madness with a grain of truth. Perhaps it is Daenerys who will wake the dragon someday.

Heroine's Journey	Book One
The World of Common Day	Daenerys dwells with her brother.
The Call To Adventure	Daenerys is promised to the Khal
Refusal of the Call	Daenerys meets Drogo and pleads to stay with her brother.
The Ruthless Mentor and the Bladeless Talisman	Ser Jorah offers comfort and advice at her wedding. He gives her books.
The Crossing of the First Threshold	Daenerys weds Drogo
Sidekicks, Trials, Adversaries	Daenerys learns to manage her brother and her husband's bloodriders as Khaleesi.
Wedding the Animus	Daenerys seduces her husband, conceives a child, and learns the prophecy her son will fulfill.
Facing Bluebeard	She deals with her brother at last.
Finding the Sensitive Man	Drogo learns tenderness.
Confronting the Powerless Father	Dany sees Drogo fall from his horse and finally die at her hand.
Descent into Darkness	Daenerys faces death during the miscarriage that threatens her life and destroys her family.
Atonement with the Mother	Mirri teaches Dany a valuable lesson about trust. Dany uses this lesson to sacrifice Mirri and walk into the fire with her dragon eggs.
Death and Rebirth. Winning the Family	Daenerys is reborn from the fire as Mother of Dragons.
The Magic Flight Reinstating the Family Return	Many of Daenerys's people abandon her, but she forms a new khalasar and travels for Westeros.

The Prophecy
In the House of the Undying, Daenerys receives a prophecy detailing the path her story will take (Martin noted at Worldcon 2012 that this was dropped from the show as producers were unclear – unlike Martin – in how this would be fulfilled and there are no guarantees the show will last until the story's end.)

> *three heads has the dragon . . .*
> *. . . three fires must you light . . . one for life and one for death and one to love . . .*
> *. . . three mounts must you ride . . . one to bed and one to dread and one to love . . .*
> *. . . three treasons will you know . . . once for blood and once for gold and once for love . . .* (II.515)

Some of the prophecy has been made clear: "The Undying of Qarth had told her she would be thrice betrayed. Mirri Maz Duur had been the first, Ser Jorah [in season one] the second," Daenerys thinks (V.38). More of the prophecy is guessable. These three heads represent a partnership – three dragonriders to share the three magical mounts. As Daenerys notes:

> The dragon has three heads. There are two men in the world who I can trust, if I can find them. I will not be alone then. We will be three against the world, like Aegon [the Conqueror] and his sisters. (III:981)

As for the three mounts, the first is Daenerys's beloved Silver, which she rode on their wedding night as she and Drogo galloped their steeds into the wilderness. The "dread" is the mightiest of her three dragons, Drogon. The fire of death will accompany it in battle or in bringing the undead Others to a true death. It's fitting that love ends each of these patterns, since if Daenerys is the foretold prince, she will need to follow in the footsteps of Azor Ahai, the first hero to forge Lightbringer:

> To fight the darkness, Azor Ahai needed to forge a hero's sword. He labored for thirty days and thirty nights until it was done. However, when he went to temper it in water, the

sword broke. He was not one to give up easily, so he started over. The second time he took fifty days and fifty nights to make the sword, even better than the first. To temper it this time, he captured a lion and drove the sword into its heart, but once more the steel shattered. The third time, with a heavy heart, for he knew beforehand what he must do to finish the blade, he worked for a hundred days and nights until it was finished. This time, he called for his wife, Nissa Nissa, and asked her to bare her breast. He drove his sword into her breast, her soul combining with the steel of the sword, creating Lightbringer. (II:115)

The fire Daenerys must light to love may be this forging, or this sacrifice may be the punishment for the love that betrays her.

Enemies and Mission

The adversary on the heroine's journey is the evil stepmother who slays the innocent, like Mirri Maz Duur. However, the heroine often faces the male heads of power as well. Daenerys defeats the patriarchy as old men in charge of the old way – cruelty and exploitation of the innocent. First are her brother and Drogo, though she only watches the former's death, and the latter is a mercy-killing.

Following this, she meets Pyat Pree in the House of the Undying – an entire edifice devoted to avoiding the cycle of life. There the withered Undying Ones rule, with violet skin from drinking shade-of-the-evening, preserved and unnatural. On the show, Pree's deep-set eyes make his face resemble a skull. They kidnap Daenerys's "children," and Daenerys's dragon "child" kills them in retribution.

After, Daenerys visits cities of Slaver's Bay, beginning with Astapor, to purchase Unsullied. When she discovers their masters make them murder babies, she ends the practice forever, killing all the "Good Masters" and freeing all the slaves of the city. She commands the Unsullied to kill the leaders and soldiers but "harm no child under twelve and strike the chains off every slave you see" (III:381). In Meereen, she kills one aristocrat for every slave child those in charge have murdered. Her enemies are the murderers of the city, even as she rules fairly and destroys the old order.

Daenerys may go on to slay more patriarchs of the old world and slavery, murderers and exploiters of the weak, but she must advance to her ultimate adversary. The heroine's greatest enemy is the destroyer of life – sometimes as a mysterious force, neither male or female, sometimes as the dark matriarch, slayer of children. The former is clearly the evil god bringing unending winter on the world, while the evil mother has more possibilities. Melisandre, birther of shadows, slayer of the life-loving Renly, is one such figure. Another is Lady Stoneheart, once a mother, who now preys on the innocent.

The ultimate evil mother of Westeros is Cersei. "From what I saw of Joffrey, you are as unfit a mother as you are a ruler," her uncle says scathingly (IV:114). Her producing the twisted Joffrey is only surpassed by the treacherous adultery that throws the succession into doubt and shatters the realm. She uses people, from her young cousin Lancel to Ros, whom she beats. Consumed by a prophecy that "Queen you shall be . . . until there comes another, younger and more beautiful, to cast you down and take all that you hold dear" (IV:540), she preys on the future queens of Westeros. Daenerys may be this young queen to cast her down.

This is Daenerys's battle in the physical world, while her more spiritual battle against the Others will guide her to light her third fire for love and pat the ultimate price for peace and salvation.

End
The heroine's journey usually ends with her triumphing over the destroyer of the innocent and becoming a mother, giving birth to our nurturing the next generation.

Can Daenerys have another child? Or is her role as Mother to the Slaves sufficient? If she is the last Targaryen, her line and dragon power may die with her. (Indeed, the children of the forest and giants are fading, so this may be magic's last gasp. Or she may restore magic and bring about a new dynasty).

"When the sun rises in the west and sets in the east," said Mirri Maz Duur. "When the seas go dry and mountains blow in the wind like leaves. When your womb quickens again, and you bear a living child. Then he [Drogo] will return, and not before" (I:635). All this seems a highly-unlikely synonym for "never." Martin comments, with regards to Daenerys's fertility, "I am sure Daenerys would like to know. Prophecy can be a tricky business."[73] This reference to prophecy suggests these words may come true in a way. From the "sun," a child of Martell, to the Dothraki sea beginning to dry and pyramids turning to ash in *A Dance with Dragons*, these conditions can be seen in the khaleesi's story arc.

The history of her relationships suggest love awaits her – after Drogo, the lord of a patriarchal, chauvinist culture who trades for her like a slave, Daenerys experiments with an untrustworthy lover, a political marriage, and occasional dalliances with her handmaid, whose kisses "tasted of duty" (II:993). The one relationship she hasn't experienced is a loving partnership of equals. Many fans believe Daenerys's vision of the blue rose on the ice wall with a pleasant scent means she'll fall for Jon, another child of destiny about her age and the possible co-heir to her Targaryen legacy. Other heroes, from Greyjoys to Targaryen claimants, seek her hand as well.

Of course, if her one true love arrives, the Azor Ahai prophecy may come to pass, for herself or for Jon, its other most likely vessel. If Jon or Dany betrays and stabs the other to reforge Lightbringer, the treason for love appears. Lightbringer would kindle a "fire to love" or possibly a cataclysm among the White Walkers. It might trap Daenerys inside it, as it did Azor's wife, or awaken a hidden warg power (a mount). Or she could reforge Lightbringer herself and push her love onto the path of sacrifice and divine fire. This would follow the heroine's death-rebirth pattern as it did at Drogo's funeral pyre.

One thing is clear: whether or not she can bear children and restore the Targaryens, Daenerys is the child of prophecy, the one who will restore the world through her fires, her dragons, and her love.

Heroine's Journey	Entire Series	Prophecy of the House of the Undying
The World of Common Day	Daenerys dwells with her brother, the Beggar King.	
The Call To Adventure	Daenerys is promised to the Khal and given the Silver	*three mounts must you ride . . . one to bed*
Refusal of the Call	Daenerys meets Drogo and pleads to stay with her brother.	
The Ruthless Mentor and the Bladeless Talisman	The Maegi teaches Daenerys about women's secret magic but ultimately betrays her in a harsh lesson.	*three treasons will you know . . . once for blood*
The Crossing of the First Threshold	Daenerys dies in the fire and is reborn as the Mother of Dragons	*three fires must you light . . . one for life*
Sidekicks, Trials, Adversaries	Daenerys conquers cities and befriends lords and knights. Ser Jorah betrays Daenerys.	*three treasons will you know . . . once for gold*
Wedding the Animus	Two princes or heroes will ride beside her, different as fire and ice, reflecting the heroine. The triple pattern of the prophecies also suggests a third husband.	*three heads has the dragon . . .*
Facing Bluebeard	Dany's second husband may be plotting her assassination.	
Finding the Sensitive Man	Barristan bemoans the fact that Daenerys chooses the handsome dazzling men over a homely, loyal youth.	

Confronting the Powerless Father	In Meereen, Dany's dragon embodies her anger at the brutal gladiator pits. Next she will face the once-frightening Dothraki.	
Descent into Darkness	Death and Dread occur in Meereen, but more destruction is coming.	*. . . three fires must you light . . . one for death…three mounts must you ride . . . one to dread*
Atonement with the Mother	Quaithe awaits in Asshai. A female adversary or the force of entropy, enemy of all life, is waiting at series climax.	
Death and Rebirth	If Azor reborn (many signs point to Jon) betrays his love, Daenerys, and stabs her (treason for love) to reforge Lightbringer, the blade's "fire to love" might trap Daenerys or kindle a warg power (a mount). Or she might reforge Lightbringer.	*…three fires must you light…one to love…three mounts must you ride . . . one to love…three treasons will you know . . . once for love . . .*
Reward: Winning the Family	Through her sacrifice, Daenerys will save the world and all her people.	
The Magic Flight Reinstating the Family, Return	Daenerys leaves the north and takes the Iron Throne at last.	
Queen of Life and Death	She weds, bears a child, or becomes the true mother of her people. Through her experiences she is a truly wise queen and khaleesi.	

THE GREAT HOUSES OF WESTEROS

House Stark

Seat: Winterfell
Motto: "Winter is Coming"
Sigil: white direwolf on grey
Symbolism: The wolf symbolizes free will, but also unity and loyalty, as they roam in packs. The wolf's ability to see in the dark makes it a symbol of instinctive knowledge. Of course, the Stark children's wolves also echo their owners – while Arya dutifully plays cupbearer, she dreams that Nymeria, named for a conqueror queen is savaging men in the forest. By contrast, Sansa's Lady, like Sansa herself, is sacrificed.

> Healthy wolves and healthy women share certain psychic characteristics. Wolves and women are relational by nature, inquiring, possessed of great endurance and strength. They are deeply intuitive, intensely concerned with their young, their mate, and their pack. They are experienced in adapting to constantly changing circumstances; they are fiercely stalwart and very brave.[74]

Looking at this list of characteristics, Arya seems to possess them all, while Sansa has none. The loss of her wolf has crippled her and kept her from her potential.

When the boys of the family are angry or in danger, it is their wolves that lash out, expressing the emotions they cannot. The wolves represent their helpful shadow sides, often feared and banished from the civilized castle, yet a force of power and intuitive awareness. All the heroes are stronger with this force beside them.

Lord Eddard "Ned" Stark

"You think my life is such a precious thing to me, that I would trade my honor for a few more years...of what?" —Ned Stark to Varys
played by Sean Bean
Ned Stark grew up with Robert Baratheon, fostered by Jon Arryn. These ties are reflected in his sons' names as well as his devotion to both men. He becomes Hand of the King and investigates Jon Arryn's murder, but is executed by Joffrey for discovering that Joffrey is a bastard and announcing it to the world. He is known for his honor, which is so inflexible that he's unskilled at playing politics.

First Ranger Benjen Stark

Ned's brother is a ranger scout. Jon considers him a mentor and follows him to the Wall. He is lost on a mission in season one, fate unknown.

Lyanna Stark

Ned's deceased sister and King Robert's beloved fiancée. She was kidnapped or ran off with crown prince Rhaegar Targaryen, inciting King Aerys to murder her protesting father and brother (Rickard and Brandon Stark) and begin the war known as Robert's Rebellion. She died just as the war was ending, under mysterious circumstances. Ned was there, and he made her an important promise. Further discussion is available in the section on Jon's parentage.

Catelyn "Cat" Stark
"All these years and I still feel like an outsider when I come here."
—*Catelyn Stark to Ned Stark in the godswood*
played by Michelle Fairley
Catelyn of House Tully was betrothed to Brandon Stark, heir to Winterfell. A jealous Petyr Baelish dueled Brandon for Catelyn's favor, and Brandon spared his life as a favor to Catelyn. After his death she wed the new Stark heir, Ned, and her sister wed Jon Arryn. Thus the three great houses joined forces for the war. Though she never likes her husband's bastard, Jon, or truly forgives her husband for bringing him home, she and Ned share a close, devoted marriage until his death and have five children together. After Ned's death, she insists on riding with Robb, though she betrays him when she attempts to trade Jaime Lannister for her daughters. Her sister is Lysa Arryn. Her brother, Edmure, is the heir to House Tully.

Jon Snow
"Kill the boy [within yourself], Jon Snow. Winter is almost upon us. Kill the boy and let the man be born." – *Maester Aemon to Jon Snow*
wolf: Ghost
played by Kit Harington
Jon Snow, seventeen, is a bastard, raised alongside the Stark children but always aware that he would not inherit. The last name Snow is given to all bastards in the north, compared with Rivers, Stone, or Sand in other regions. He resolves to never have a bastard and give him such a life. He's always intended to go to the Wall, and when his father leaves, he does. There, he's made steward to the Lord Commander and groomed to replace him. Jon goes out ranging with Qhorin Halfhand, who insists Jon kill him and get himself adopted into Mance Rayder's camp to spy for the Night's Watch. There, Jon finds himself drawn to the wildling girl Ygritte as he decides where his loyalties lie.

Robb Stark. "The Young Wolf"
"My father is dead. And the only parent I have left has no right to call anyone reckless."
wolf: Grey Wind
played by Richard Madden
The eldest Stark son, age seventeen. He isn't as perceptive as he should be, as he often fails to heed Grey Wind's warnings. Though betrothed to a Frey girl, he falls in love and marries, offending the Freys. He wins three battles against the Lannisters and captures Jaime, impressing everyone with his success in the field.

Talisa Maegyr Stark
"I decided two things that day. I would not waste my years planning dances and masquerades with the other noble ladies. And when I came of age I would never live in a slave city again."
played by Oona Chaplin
Talisa Maegyr Stark, a healer from the Free Cities, falls in love with Robb and marries him in season two. Robb's wife in the book, Jeyne Westerling, is much weaker, with only a docile, "sweet" personality. She's terrified of Grey Wind. As more of her courtship with Robb appeared onscreen (the section in the book is from Catelyn's point of view, and she only finds out after the wedding) the character moved further away from Jeyne's. When she gained a Volantene heritage and backstory, Martin renamed her something more fitting.

Sansa Stark
"Courtesy is a lady's armor"
wolf: Lady, killed by Ned on King Robert's orders.
played by Sophie Turner
Stark's eldest daughter, 13-year-old Sansa lives as if she's in a ballad or romance. She wants a beautiful marriage with a handsome prince or knight. She's swept away by handsome Joffrey and has a deep crush on Ser Loras, the gorgeous champion of the tournaments. She dislikes those she thinks are ugly, like Tyrion. As she's held captive in King's Landing, she

comes to see the value of people beneath the surface – in the book, Ser Dontos, whom she saves by making a jester (in 2.1) vows his life to her service in a picture of courtly love. Most characters see her as a pawn, for with Bran and Rickon vanished, if Robb dies childless, Sansa is his heir.

Arya Stark
"Stick 'em with the pointy end!"
wolf: Nymeria, named for a warrior-queen
played by Maisie Williams
Feisty 11-year-old tomboy who doesn't want to do needlepoint. Instead she wants to use weapons and fight. Jon, who loves her deeply, gives her a sword she names Needle, for as she says, "Sansa has her needle and I have mine." She trains in dueling with Syrio Forel, the swordmaster from Braavos. When her father is arrested, Syrio (presumably) dies defending her, and Arya escapes the keep. She witnesses her father's death and escapes with the recruits for the Night's Watch. At Harrenhal, the Faceless Man Jaqen H'ghar agrees to kill three men for her, and after she finagles her escape, he offers her a password that will take her to the Faceless Men in Braavos. After various adventures, she and her friends Gendry and Hot Pie escape their captivity at Harrenhal and meet the Brotherhood without Banners, who take Arya captive, along with Sandor Clegane.

Arya's Companions

Gendry
played by Joe Dempsie
An unacknowledged bastard of King Robert, Gendry becomes a blacksmith's apprentice and makes a fine bull's head helmet. He joins the Watch, then becomes Arya's companion to Harrenhal and the Brotherhood Without Banners, whom he's interested in joining.

Hot Pie
played by Ben Hawkey
A humble baker's boy originally bound for the Wall, Hot Pie follows Arya on her adventures and escapes

from Harrenhal with her, though he finally settles down to be a baker.

Bran Stark

"Can a man still be brave if he's afraid?" – Bran Stark
"That is the only time a man can be brave." – Eddard Stark
played by Isaac Hempstead
wolf: Summer
A ten-year-old who loves climbing, until Jaime Lannister pushes him off a wall. Though crippled, he learns to ride and is carried about by the large lackwit, Hodor. In the first season someone sends an assassin after him, which might or might not have been employed by the Lannisters.

Bran's Companions

Hodor
played by Kristian Nairn
Hodor, a lackwit, can only utter his one signature word. He's strong enough to carry Bran on his adventures, however.

Jojen Reed
"Dreams are what we have."
played by Thomas Brodie-Sangster
Jojen has true dreams and knows much of how to be a warg, who rides in the minds of animals. He seeks Bran out to be his friend and tutor. In the books, the siblings are visiting Winterfell to pledge fealty, and escape with Bran during Theon's attack, while in the show they arrive in the third season.

Meera Reed
played by Ellie Kendrick
Meera is Jojen's warrior sibling, with spear, knife and net. Their father, Howland Reed, rules the Neck. He was a Bannerman and close friend of Ned Stark's.

Osha
"You tell him this, m'lord. You tell him he's bound on marching the wrong way. It's north he should be taking his swords. North, not south. You hear me?" – Osha, to Bran, regarding Robb.
played by Natalia Tena
Osha is a wildling who travels south fleeing Mance Rayder but is captured by the Starks. She knows much about the Old Ways and advises Bran. When Winterfell is destroyed, she helps Bran and Rickon escape and accompanies them on their travels.

Rickon Stark
wolf: Shaggydog
He's just six, and acts increasingly savagely as more of his family leave Winterfell, abandoning him as he sees it. One scene has him smashing nuts savagely with a rock while Bran tries to govern. Rickon dreams of his father's death, as he shares his brother's prophetic dreams. When Winterfell is destroyed, he escapes with Bran and Osha.

See Theon Greyjoy, ward and hostage of the Starks, page 152

House Stark Retainers
Rodrik Cassel
played by Ron Donachie
Ser Rodrik Cassel is Master-at-Arms at Winterfell. He's executed by Theon Greyjoy during the castle's fall.

Jory Cassel
played by Jamie Sives
The captain of the guards and nephew of Ser Rodrik, he accompanies Ned to King's Landing and is killed defending him from Jaime Lannister.

Maester Luwin
played by Donald Sumpter
The healer and wise guide of the castle and a close advisor of Bran's. After Theon's attack, he dies in the Godswood.

Vayon Poole
The steward of Winterfell and father of Sansa's best friend, Jeyne

Jeyne Poole
Jeyne Poole, Sansa's best friend, is ladylike and courtly like she is. She accompanies her to the Capitol, where (on the show) they attend the Tournament of the Hand together. When Ned Stark is arrested, the Lannisters capture Jeyne and lock her up. In the book, an imprisoned Sansa only sees her friend once in King's Landing. However, the Lannisters find a use for her...

Septa Mordane
played by Susan Brown
A dour chaperone for Arya and Sansa, she accompanies the girls to King's Landing. After Ned is killed, Joffrey has her head placed on a spike.

Old Nan
played by Margaret John
The oldest person at Winterfell. Hodor is her great-grandson. The character is said to have passed away after season one to mirror the actress's passing.

House Tully

Seat: Riverrun
Sigil: a silver trout leaping on a blue and red striped field
Motto: "Family, Duty, Honor."
Symbolism: Trout signify growing prosperity. They along with salmon, appeared on Celtic coins, scepters, and so on, echoing the trout's importance as a staple.[75] The hero Fionn MacCumhail tastes the salmon or sometimes the trout of wisdom, which becomes the source of his great magic and luck. It's said, however, that if one's trout falls back into the water, a person will have a short season of happiness. In fact, one prophetess sees Catelyn in the water – after her and Robb's many triumphs, doom is approaching:

> "I dreamt of a roaring river and a woman that was a fish. Dead she drifted, with red tears on her cheeks, but when her eyes did open, oh, I woke from terror. All this I dreamt, and more." (III:249)

Eating and killing trout is occasionally taboo in Celtic legend. There's one tale of a beautiful white trout from the Otherworld, and the man who kills it is cursed forever.[76] The Freys may have a similar fate coming in the future.

Lord Tully
Lord Hoster Tully, father of Catelyn Stark and Lysa Arryn, is getting on in years and rather ill. He dies in the second episode of season three. In the book, Catelyn is with him at his death, and hears some of his greatest regrets about his daughter Lysa.

Brynden Blackfish
played by Clive Russell
Lord Hoster Tully's younger brother. Lord Tully sought to wed his brother Ser Brynden, hero of the War of the Ninepenny Kings to Bethany Redwyne, but Brynden would have none of it. This began a years-long quarrel between the two, for which Brynden earned the nickname "Blackfish," like the black sheep of the family. He's seen at his brother's funeral, counseling Catelyn and Edmure.

Ser Edmure Tully

Catelyn's brother and heir to House Tully. In the War of the Five Kings, he declares allegiance to his nephew Robb Stark. He appears in the third season, trying haplessly to light his father's funeral pyre, and then confessing to Robb that he wrecked the young king's strategy on the battlefield. He's young and not terribly able. However, he reluctantly agrees to wed a Frey girl to save Robb's campaign and regain the Frey alliance. His wife will not be a queen, but she will be the Freys' liege lord in a splendid match.

See Catelyn Stark page 135

See Lysa Arryn page 155

House Baratheon
Seat: Storm's End
Sigil: A crowned black stag rampant on a gold field
Motto: "Ours is the Fury"
Symbolism: To the Celts, the stag was king of the forest and the key to the people's survival. Of course, it is also an herbivore, a creature ill-equipped to battle lions and wolves.

King Robert Baratheon
"I was never so alive as when I was winning this throne, or so dead as now that I've won it."
played by Mark Addy
When young, he was fostered with Lord Jon Arryn at the Eyrie along with Ned Stark, and he grew to consider them his own family. He was betrothed to Ned's sister Lyanna. When Rhaegar kidnapped her, Robert eventually slew him and claimed the throne in what is known as "Robert's Rebellion." With Lyanna dead, he married Cersei Lannister for political reasons. When he took the throne, he gave Stannis the isle of Dragonstone and Renly the Baratheon seat of Storm's End. His officially acknowledged children are Joffrey, Myrcella, and Tommen Baratheon, though Ned Stark discovers all three are not truly his. Around the time of Ned's discovery, Cersei's cousin and Robert's squire, Lancel Lannister, gives him too much strongwine while hunting and he's mortally wounded by a boar.

Robert's Bastards
According to a prophecy in the series, King Robert sired sixteen bastards. They have not all been seen in the books. Varys, for instance, says he knows of ten.
The only bastards seen on the show are Gendry and the baby Barra. In the books, Robert only acknowledges one bastard, and the rest appear ignorant of their parentage. He conceived Edric Storm with Lady Delena Florent in his brother Stannis's wedding bed, and fostered the boy at Storm's End. Gendry inherits Edric Storm's plot, as Melisandre in the third book seeks to execute a king's son but Stannis is reluctant.

Other bastards in the books include Mya Stone, a capable guide for visitors in the Eyrie, the adult brothel girl Bella (whom Gendry almost sleeps with!), and a pair of twins at Casterly Rock. All that could be found (not including Gendry, Edric, Bella, or Mya) are executed by Joffrey, to ensure they can't claim the throne.

Stannis Baratheon

"I dream of it sometimes. Of Renly's dying. A green tent, candles, a woman screaming. And blood. I was still abed when he died. Your Devan will tell you. He tried to wake me. Dawn was nigh and my lords were waiting, fretting. I should have been ahorse, armored. I knew Renly would attack at break of day. Devan says I thrashed and cried out, but what does it matter? It was a dream. I was in my tent when Renly died, and when I woke my hands were clean." – Stannis Baratheon to Davos Seaworth.

played by Stephen Dillane

Stannis is ruler of Dragonstone. Following his brother's death, he seeks the throne for himself, but he is famously unpopular. His association with the Red Priestess and insistence that people convert to her religion doesn't help matters. His daughter and heir Shireen is sickly with grayscale, and he doesn't care much for his wife Queen Selyse, of House Florent.

Stannis' Household
Red Priestess Melisandre
"The night is dark and full of terrors."
played by Carice van Houten

Melisandre is a Red Priestess of the Lord of Light. She comes from Asshai in Essos, and is a Maegi. She has gifts of healing (or at least is immune to poison) and prophecy. After beginning an affair with Stannis, she births a shadow-creature that kills King Renly. She appears to be a fanatic, who has Stannis and his wife firmly under her control.

Davos Seaworth, "The Onion Knight"
"Stannis is my god."
played by Liam Cunningham
Ser Davos Seaworth, a reformed smuggler, was born in the slums of King's Landing and remained illiterate until recent events. During Robert's Rebellion, Davos smuggled onions and other food to Stannis, who was besieged at Storm's End. Stannis rewarded Davos with knighthood and lands, but cut off his fingers as punishment for smuggling. Davos wore the fingerbones around his neck as a lucky charm until he lost them at Blackwater Bay. As Stannis's Hand, he is utterly loyal, though he's more suspicious of Melisandre. Davos and his wife Marya have seven sons in the book: Dale, Allard, Matthos, Maric, Devan, Stannis and Steffon. The oldest four are killed at Blackwater Bay and the youngest two live with their mother. Devan is Stannis's devoted page. On the show, Matthos dies at Blackwater and the others are unmentioned.

Queen Selyse Florent
played by Tara Fitzgerald
Stannis and his wife have a loveless marriage, but she is a true fanatic of the Lord of Light, who originally introduced Stannis and the Red Priestess. She dwells in a tower on Dragonstone, consumed by her thoughts.

Princess Shireen
played by Kerry Ingram
Selyse and Stannis have one daughter, Shireen, who is disfigured by the disease called greyscale, which turns skin to stone. She's nine in the first book and considered sweet but not pretty. She hides away from people and is an avid reader.

Renly Baratheon
"You may well have the better claim, but I have the larger army." *–Renly to Stannis*
played by Gethin Anthony
Renly is known for being handsome and charming, more like Robert than Stannis. When he dies, killed by Melisandre's shadow creature, Renly is married to Margaery Tyrell and having an affair with her brother, Ser Loras Tyrell. He is also trying to claim the Iron Throne.

Joffrey Baratheon
"We've had vicious kings and we've had idiot kings, but I don't know if we've ever been cursed with a vicious idiot for a king." *–Tyrion to Joffrey*
played by Jack Gleeson
The heir apparent, then king of Westeros, Joffrey is bloodthirsty and cruel underneath his handsome face. He chooses his whims over politics.

Myrcella Baratheon
"One day I pray you love someone. I pray you love her so much when you close your eyes you see her face. I want that for you. I want you to know what it's like to love someone, to truly love someone, before I take her from you." *–Cersei to Tyrion, in her grief over parting with Myrcella*
played by Aimee Richardson
In personality, she's sweet, kind, and tractable, including to people Joffrey mocks, like Sansa and Tyrion. Tyrion, who regards her with affection, betroths her to the youngest prince of Dorne and sends her there, out of the war. So far, she's displayed little dialogue or personality and is treated as a pawn.

Tommen Baratheon
played by Callum Wharry
Tommen Baratheon is placid, friendly, and rather useless in tournaments or politics. He's also sweet and kind. Joffrey berates him for crying at parting from his sister and for incompetence on the training field. He mostly does what everyone tells him.

House Lannister
Seat: Casterly Rock
Sigil: A golden lion rampant on a crimson field
Motto: "Hear Me Roar!"
Symbolism: The lion of course is a royal symbol, often seen on heraldry. It is a symbol of power, majesty, courage and strength. Among the Celts it represented warrior gatherings much as the dragon did.[77] Like the lion, the Lannisters have their savage side – Tywin wiped out House Castamere for its pride, as detailed in the popular Westerosi song, "The Rains of Castamere."

Tywin Lannister
"A lion doesn't concern himself with the opinions of a sheep."
played by Charles Dance
Tywin rules Casterly Rock and is appointed Hand of the King for Joffrey. Previously, he was Mad King Aerys' hand and betrayed him to his death. He appears devoted to Jaime and filled with loathing for Tyrion, while he treats Cersei with sexist contempt. These feelings seriously motivate the personalities of his three children.

Jaime Lannister "The Kingslayer"
"So many vows … they make you swear and swear. Defend the king. Obey the king. Keep his secrets. Do his bidding. Your life for his. But obey your father. Love your sister. Protect the innocent. Defend the weak. Respect the gods. Obey the laws. It's too much. No matter what you do, you're forsaking one vow or another."
played by Nikolaj Coster-Waldau
At a legendary fifteen, Jaime was the best fighter of his age. While his father intended Jaime to wed Lysa Tully, Cersei suggested to Jaime that he instead join the Kingsguard of the Mad King Aerys and be close to her forever in King's Landing, where their father was Hand. Jaime joined, against his father's wishes, but Tywin resigned as Hand in a fury and dragged Cersei back to Casterly Rock. The twins (already lovers) were parted once more.

In court, Jaime became increasingly conflicted, when for instance, he heard the king raping the queen and didn't know whom to protect. Forced to watch savage executions as the Starks were burned alive, he learned to go away inside himself so he didn't have to face the king's actions.

As Aerys was losing the war, he planned to burn the city with wildfire. When Tywin arrived at the head of an army, Aerys ordered Jaime to execute him. Seeing no right choice, Jaime slew Aerys instead. Jaime sat on the Iron Throne, but willingly offered it to Ned Stark when he arrived. Robert forgave Jaime and kept him for his Kingsguard. While living close to his sister, Robert's new queen, Jaime fathered Joffrey, Myrcella, and Tommen with her.

He's a celebrated warrior, brilliant on the battlefield but weak at politics. He tries to be honorable in his own way and has slept with no one but Cersei. However, his legacy as Kingslayer follows him. In his first episode, he establishes his personality by pushing Bran to his likely death, but Jaimie's vulnerability and conflicted duty grow more apparent through the series. Likewise, being escorted towards King's Landing by Brienne, the soul of honor, changes him to a better person.

Cersei Lannister
"Love only your children."
played by Lena Headey
Cersei is ambitious and cunning, but also irrational and over-emotional. Her mothering turns Joffrey into a monster. (The younger two siblings seem pleasant but ineffectually obedient.) Politically, she's too determined to win every confrontation, whatever the consequences later. "She does not lack for wits, but she has no judgment and no patience," Jaime thinks (IV:234). She's jealous of many characters, including the younger Sansa and Margaery. Her failure to control them, Joffrey, or the courtiers begins to erode her power.

She truly loves her brother Jaime and her children, though she resents it when any of them contradict her wishes or disobey her. Tyrion she loathes. From childhood, she's been driven by a particular prophecy, as well as her desire to be with Jaime. However, she failed to love Robert Baratheon mostly because he cared more for dead Lyanna Stark than for her. She kills any child of his she carries, and cuckolds him with her brother, beginning the destruction of the realm. When Jaime is captured, she begins an affair with her cousin Lancel.

Tyrion Lannister "The Imp"
"Those are brave men knocking at our door. Let's go kill them!"
played by Peter Dinklage
Tyrion Lannister is the youngest child of Tywin and Joanna, who died giving birth to him. Tyrion is a dwarf, mockingly called The Imp and The Halfman. Knowing that he could not be a warrior, he chose to cultivate his mind and witty tongue, though he performs heroically at the Battle of Blackwater Bay. Jaime cares for him, though Cersei and Joffrey do not.

Tyrion's Household

Podrick Payne
played by Daniel Portman
Podrick Payne is a cousin of Ser Ilyn Payne, the King's Justice. As Tyrion's squire, he longs to be a knight. He obeys Tyrion devotedly and brings reinforcements during the Battle of Blackwater. He personally saves Tyrion from Ser Mandon Moore's assassination attempt. Apparently, he's very desirable to the ladies.

Bronn
Tyrion: And here we have Bronn, son of...
Bronn: You wouldn't know him.
played by Jerome Flynn
Bronn is a deadly sellsword working for Tyrion. When Catelyn captures Tyrion at the inn, Bronn goes along, and defends Tyrion in Lysa's trial by combat. By fighting dishonorably, he wins, and Tyrion decides to keep him on. In King's Landing, Tyrion appoints him Commander of the City Watch in place of slimy Janos Slynt. In season three, Bronn is rewarded with a knighthood for his contribution during "Blackwater."

Shae
played by Sibel Kekilli
Shae hails from the Free Cities and works as a prostitute before Tyrion adopts her into his household while he's fighting alongside his father. They develop a sincere affection for each other (or so it appears), so much so that he smuggles her to King's Landing. He eventually hides her as Sansa's lady-in-waiting (a position she doesn't get in the books until Sansa marries).

Ser Kevan Lannister
played by Ian Gelder
Ser Kevan Lannister is his brother Tywin's loyal adviser. While he's mostly seen in the background, he will have a larger role to play when there are fewer Lannisters. His sons include Lancel (below) and the young Lannister killed by Rickard Karstark.

Alton Lannister
played by Karl Davies
Alton Lannister is captured by Robb alongside his cousin Ser Jaime Lannister. He is sent back and forth delivering peace terms until Jamie Lannister murders him to aid in an escape attempt. Jaime then kills Torrhen Karstark, his guard. In the book, a Frey cousin to the Lannisters has his role.

Lancel Lannister
"Tell my friend Bronn to please kill you if anything should happen to me."
"Please kill me if anything should happen to Lord Tyrion."
"It will be my pleasure."
played by Eugene Simon
This young, handsome squire was sent to King's Landing by Tywin Lannister to serve as King Robert's squire, and after, to serve the queen. Without Jaime around, Cersei convinces Lancel to "serve" her in more personal ways. Tyrion figures this out and demands Lancel spy for him.

House Greyjoy
Seat: Pyke
Sigil: A golden kraken on a black field.
Motto: "We Do Not Sow."
Symbolism: Krakens, popular from *Pirates of the Caribbean, Clash of the Titans,* and Sinbad the Sailor, are mythical giant squids. The Kraken signifies a watery death for anything that travels too close as it lurks unseen, king of the waters, though helpless on land.

Balon Greyjoy
"No man gives me a crown. I pay the iron price. I will take my crown."
played by Patrick Malahide
Balon Greyjoy is the Lord of the Iron Islands and the head of House Greyjoy. Balon and his wife Alannys of House Harlaw had four children: Rodrik, Maron, Yara/Asha and Theon. Years ago, he rebelled against the Iron Throne, and Ned Stark killed Balon's older two sons in battle and took Theon home with him as a hostage. Under Balon's rule, his people begin a campaign against the North in season two, seizing many castles while Robb's in the South, fighting. Stannis and Melisandre curse Balon to death near the end of season three, along with Joffrey and Robb.

Alannys Greyjoy
This daughter of House Harlaw (a subordinate house to the Greyjoys) has been staying at Harlaw for her health—the loss of two sons and capture of the third has driven her nearly mad. Her brother, Lord Rodrik Harlaw, called Rodrik the Reader, has a special affection for Yara/Asha Greyjoy.

Balon's Brothers
Euron Greyjoy, called the Crow's Eye, is exiled after dishonoring Victarion's wife and sails far to the east. Victarion Greyjoy is the Lord Captain of the Iron Fleet. Aeron Greyjoy, the youngest brother, became a priest of the Drowned God (in the second book, he's the priest who rededicates Theon). They feature heavily in the fourth book.

Theon Greyjoy
Maester Luwin: You're not the man you're pretending to be.
Theon: You may be right, old man. But I've gone too far to pretend to be
anything else.
played by Alfie Allen

Theon Greyjoy spent half his life as Ned Stark's ward and hostage. He saw Ned as not terribly cruel but somewhat distant, as Ned always remained aware he might need to execute his hostage someday. Theon likes Robb, whom he sees as a younger brother. When Theon fails to convince his father to support Robb in his rebellion, he captures Winterfell in an attempt to prove his worth. He soon loses the fortress, after allegedly executing Bran and Rickon Stark. The Bastard of Bolton carries him off and tortures him. Until the fifth book arrived, readers were unsure of Theon's precise fate, and his appearances in season three were told only in flashback.

Yara Greyjoy
(called Asha in the books)
played by Gemma Whelan

Yara is a warrior and captain, which is unusual for women on the isles. She also wishes to be declared her father's heir. Yara, more capable and better-regarded than Theon, is assigned thirty ships to seize the northern castle Deepwood Motte while Theon is given only a single ship. Her name was switched to avoid confusion with Osha the wildling, but her plot arc and character appear unchanged.

House Tyrell

Seat: Highgarden
Sigil: Golden rose on a green field
Motto: "Growing Strong"
Symbolism: When golden roses were first introduced to Europe, they symbolized jealousy and fading affection. A gift of such a rose meant the relationship was doomed. This seems rather fitting for Margaery.

Lord Mace Tyrell

The Lord of Highgarden fights little and is more interested in political alliance. He's eager for his daughter to be queen.

Loras Tyrell

played by Finn Jones
Ser Loras is an impressive tournament knight. In the book, he's the third son of Lord Mace; on the show he appears to be the heir. He is the lover of Lord Renly Baratheon.

Margaery Tyrell

"If Renly wasn't a king then I'm not a queen."
"Do you want to be a queen?"
"No. I want to be THE queen."
played by Natalie Dormer
Lady Margaery married Renly, and didn't even object to his affairs with her brother. Following Renly's death, Margaery is betrothed to King Joffrey Baratheon. She is adroit at manipulating others, even Joffrey.

Lady Olenna

played by Diana Rigg
Lady Olenna is Lord Mace's mother and Margaery's grandmother. She's irreverent and clever, and appears to be the schemer of House Tyrell.

House Martell
Rulers of the Kingdom of Dorne
Seat: Sunspear
Motto: "Unbowed, unbent, unbroken"
Sigil: a sun with a spear through it
Symbolism: The sun represents the pinnacle of spiritual development and human achievement. This is a sad reflection on Quentyn Martell, but perhaps Dorne has great battle successes to come.

In the show, little has been seen of Dorne: Prince Rhaegar's wife Elia came from there, and Princess Myrcella Baratheon is sent there to cement an alliance and for her protection. She's betrothed to Prince Trystane Martell. In book four, more of the southernmost kingdom is seen.

Doran Nymeros Martell
Doran Martell is the Prince of Dorne and Lord of Sunspear. Afflicted by gout, he enjoys watching the young children play in the water gardens. He avoids declaring his allegiance in the War of the Five Kings until the Lannisters send Myrcella Baratheon to wed his son Trystane, promise justice for the murder of his sister Elia, and give him a seat on the Small Council.

Doran's Children
His heir, Arianne Martell, is still unmarried. His younger sons are Quentyn and Trystane Martell.

Prince Oberyn Nymeros Martell "The Red Viper"
Prince Doran's last surviving sibling, Prince Oberyn is very hot-tempered. His nickname comes from rumors of his poisoned blade.

Oberyn's Children
He has eight bastard daughters, called the Sand Snakes, who are each uniquely vicious and cunning.

House Arryn

Seat: The Eyrie

Sigil: White hawk and crescent

Motto: "As High as Honor"

Symbolism: The hawk signifies swiftness and keen sight – in fact, Jon Arryn was one of few to discover Cersei's infidelity. It is also a hunter and tracker, as Jon proved in the Capitol, until those abilities killed him. Of course, the hawk also is reflected in the inaccessible height of the Eyrie. While the hawk is a masculine symbol, the crescent moon, by contrast, is feminine. However, the symbolism is barren, as the Godswood is dead and the Eyrie icy, pale stone.

Jon Arryn

Jon Arryn was Lord of the Eyrie and Hand of the King to Robert Baratheon. Years earlier, Jon fostered Eddard Stark and Robert Baratheon as his wards in the Vale and loved them as his sons. His sudden death led to Ned's appointment and investigation of his murder. It seems clear that Jon became aware that Joffrey and his siblings were bastards, so he was executed by the Lannisters before he could talk. However, Lysa knows more than she's told.

Lysa Arryn

played by Kate Dickie

Jon's widow and Catelyn's sister appears irrational and fearful. Lysa was raised at Riverrun as a girl of the highborn Tully family. After her much-older husband's death, she retreats to the Eyrie with her young son and refuses to leave or to send troops to her nephew Robb's rebellion. In the books, she's Jon's third wife, as the previous two had not produced children. Her marriage to Jon was political and largely loveless. It produced one sickly son.

Robin/Robert Arryn

"Can I make the little man fly now?"

played by Lino Facioli

On the show, Robert Arryn is renamed Robin Arryn to avoid

confusion with King Robert Baratheon. The boy, still breastfeeding, is disturbingly close to his mother. He takes a hysterical glee in people's deaths and seems unstable and bloodthirsty, rather like Joffrey. His father Jon was considering sending their son to be fostered with Stannis, while King Robert favored the Lannisters for this task. Catelyn also offers to foster him and Lysa refuses with anger.

Noble Houses

House Tarth
Vassals to House Baratheon
Sigil: Yellow suns on rose quartered with white crescents on azure

Lord Selwyn Tarth
The aging head of the house

Brienne of Tarth
played by Gwendoline Christie
She is desperate to be part of King Renly Baratheon's Kingsguard, and wins a tournament to accomplish this. Though implicated in Renly's murder, she idolizes him. As they flee, Catelyn Stark adopts her as bodyguard. As season two ends, Catelyn orders her to deliver Jaime Lannister to King's Landing, in return for Sansa and Arya. Brienne and Jaime become increasingly close when they're captured by Lord Bolton's men.

House Frey
Vassals to House Tully
Sigil: Two grey towers

Walder Frey, "The Late Lord Frey,"
played by David Bradley
The Lord of the Crossing has been nicknamed "The Late Lord Frey" for his lengthy stalling when ordered to support his liege with troops, both in Robert's Rebellion and the recent wars. He has been married eight times and has roughly a hundred descendants. All are eager to inherit and most name their children Walda or Walder to curry favor. Their two towers, called the Twins, are located strategically in the Riverlands. When Robb needs to cross, his mother negotiates that he will marry a Frey daughter.

House Florent
Vassals to House Tyrell
Sigil: Fox and Flowers
House Florent follows House Tyrell in supporting Robert's youngest brother, Renly, but switches to Stannis on Renly's death. The Florents make up most of Stannis's remaining army after the Battle of Blackwater.

Lord Alester Florent
Lord Alester Florent, the head of the House Florent, is Samwell Tarly's grandfather through his daughter Melessa Florent. On Dragonstone, Alester joins his niece Queen Selyse and his brother Ser Axell in fervently following the Lord of Light.

Selyse Baratheon, formerly Florent, is Stannis's wife (page 145).

House Karstark
Vassals to House Stark
Sigil: White sunburst on black
The Karstarks, a cadet branch and kin to House Stark, follow Robb into war. When prisoner Jaime kills young Torrhen Karstark, his guard, the boy's father Lord Rickard Karstark is horrified. His other son Eddard Karstark is slain in the war. Lord Rickard demands the death of two young Lannister prisoners in turn. When he executes them in the night, Robb beheads him and his troops desert. Lord Rickard has a daughter, Alys, who has her own subplot in the later books, when she and her uncle Arnolf Karstark fight for control of their lands.

House Bolton
Vassals to House Stark
Sigil: The flayed man

Lord Roose Bolton
Robb's bannerman, traveling with him on campaign. He fought at the Trident, long ago. In the second book, he and his men capture Harrenhal from the Lannisters, and he is the one to

employ Arya as cupbearer, not Tywin Lannister. She doesn't reveal herself to him, as she's not certain of his loyalty. He weds "Fat Walda" Frey, who brings a dowry as large as she is.

The Bastard of Bolton

Ramsay Snow, his father's only living child, stays behind at the Dreadfort when his father leaves with Robb. Ramsay poisoned his trueborn brother Domeric and so became his father's heir. When Theon attacks Winterfell, Ramsay's father sends him to reclaim it for the Starks.

Ramsay is a sadist; he is cruel, savage and wild, taking delight in torturing others. He is quite fond of the old Bolton custom of flaying their enemies alive – "During the Age of Heroes, the Boltons used to flay the Starks and wear their skins as cloaks," as Jaime notes (III:845).

The second book features a subplot about "The Bastard of Bolton" that forces Robb to reconcile his bannermen while fighting for kingship: When House Hornwood loses its lord and his heir, Ramsay takes the keep and marries the widowed lady by force. He locks her in a tower without food, where's she's rumored to have eaten her own fingers before starving to death. Robb's other bannermen are appalled. Ser Rodrik Cassel attempts to stop Ramsay, but he cleverly escapes and aids Theon in his attack on Winterfell before turning on him in turn.

Locke

Locke is a man of House Bolton who captures Jaime Lannister and Brienne in the third season. He agrees to not let Brienne be raped by his men, in return for a generous ransom, but he chops off Jaime's hand. In the novels, Locke is instead the character Vargo Hoat "the Goat" who leads the Brave Companions, a group of sellswords hired (ironically) by Tywin Lannister to pillage the Riverlands before they switch sides to aid House Bolton.

House Tarly
Vassals of House Tyrell
Sigil: Red huntsman on green

Lord Randyll Tarly
A military commander and man so cruel he offered to kill Sam if his bookish eldest son refused to take the Black. In the book series, young Sam considered being a Maester, and Lord Tarly put heavy chains on him to punish him.

Melessa Tarly
Lady Tarly, formerly Florent, appears kind and loving toward Sam. The book mentions multiple daughters as well.

See Samwell Tarly under Night's Watch, page 167

Dickon Tarly
Sam's younger, more capable brother. Now the heir to his father's lands.

House Clegane
"I like dogs better than knights. My father's father was kennelmaster at the Rock. One autumn year, Lord Tytos came between a lioness and her prey. Lioness didn't give a shit that she was Lannister's own sigil. Bitch tore into my lord's horse and would have done for my lord too, but my grandfather came up with the hounds. Three of his dogs died running her off. My grandfather lost a leg, so Lannister paid him for it with lands and a towerhouse, and took his son to squire. The three dogs on our banner are the three that died, in the yellow of autumn grass. A hound will die for you, but never lie to you. And he'll look you straight in the face." (Sandor Clegane, II:262)

Vassals of House Lannister
Sigil: Three black dogs on a dark yellow background

Ser Gregor Clegane, "The Mountain That Rides."

played by Conan Stevens (season one) and Ian Whyte (season two)

Ser Gregor is a tremendously large knight, almost eight feet in height and notoriously cruel. Though Rhaegar Targaryen knighted him at Tywin Lannister's urging, Gregor murdered Rhaegar Targaryen's family, raping his wife Elia Martell and smashing in the head of their baby, Aegon, during Robert's Rebellion. During the War of the Five Kings he raids the Riverlands and kills entire villages. On the show, he's first seen killing Jon Arryn's former squire brutally in a tournament. While King's Hand, Ned demands Ser Gregor's execution for his slaughters in the Riverlands, but Ned himself is soon put on trial. Gregor Clegane rules Harrenhal for a short time, and then abandons it, slaughtering all the prisoners.

Sandor Clegane, "The Hound"

"There are no true knights, no more than there are gods. If you can't protect yourself, die and get out of the way of those who can. Sharp steel and strong arms rule this world, don't ever believe any different."

played by Rory McCann

When Sandor and Gregor were children Gregor held his brother's face in a fire, horrifically scarring him. He is the personal bodyguard of Joffrey Baratheon and does the young prince's dirty work. Sandor looks down on romance, so he refuses to be knighted, as he knows what brutes living knights can be. He has a quiet affection for Sansa Stark and rescues her from an angry mob. He offers to take her home, though she declines. King Joffrey relieves Barristan the Bold as leader of the Kingsguard so he can make Ser Jaime its leader. He then appoints Sandor to their ranks, but Sandor deserts his position during the Battle of the Blackwater, as the fires still terrify him. He's captured in the third season by the Brotherhood Without Banners.

House Mormont
Vassals of House Stark
Sigil: Black bear in a green wood

Lord Commander Jeor "The Old Bear" Mormont
When Mormont took the black, he became Lord Commander of the Night's Watch, in time. He holds the Mormont ancestral sword Longclaw, which he gives to Jon.

Ser Jorah Mormont
Jorah, Lord Jeor's son, was exiled by Ned Stark for selling his prisoners as slaves instead of sending them to the Wall. He now serves Daenerys overseas.

Maege Mormont
With her brother on the Wall and his son in exile, Maege assumes control of her House in the book (she hasn't been mentioned in the show). She and her warrior daughters ride to battle in full armor for King Robb.

King's Landing
The Small Council
Petyr "Littlefinger" Baelish
"I did warn you not to trust me."
played by Aidan Gillen
Petyr Baelish grew up as a ward of Catelyn's father, Lord Tully. As heir to a minor holding on the smallest of the Fingers (a set of small peninsulas), he's nicknamed "Littlefinger." As a young man, he loved Catelyn, but her father intended her to wed Brandon Stark (Ned's older brother before King Aerys killed him). Petyr challenged the older, stronger Brandon to a duel, and Brandon left him scarred and humiliated but alive at Catelyn's insistence. Today, Petyr brags that he slept with Catelyn and her sister Lysa, but many dismiss this as idle boasting. He is the Master of Coin on the Small Council but gathers intelligence mainly through his brothels. After urging Ned to compromise with the Lannisters, he finally sides with

King Joffrey and betrays Ned in the throne room when Ned tries to seize power.

Following the Battle of Blackwater Bay, King Joffrey names Littlefinger the Lord of Harrenhal, and liege lord to the rebellious Tullys, Catelyn's family. Though the symbol of his family is the head of the Titan of Braavos, Littlefinger's personal sigil is the harmless-looking but always singing mockingbird. He has a disturbing obsession with Sansa, who resembles her mother.

Varys, The Spider

"The storms come and go, the waves crash overhead, the big fish eat the little fish, and I keep on paddling."
played by Conleth Hill.

Varys is a eunuch and the Master of Whisperers on the king's small council. He is a skilled manipulator and commands a network of informants across two continents. Born in the Free Cities, he maintains a close partnership with Illyrio. Unlike Baelish, Varys insists he's working for the betterment of the kingdom.

Grand Maester Pycelle

The Maester of King's Landing is rather a coward. While Littlefinger and Varys are too clever to be caught, Pycelle is discovered in several schemes and betrayals. Tyrion has his beard cut off and throws him in the cells as a punishment, though he's released later.

Janos Slynt

"I'm not questioning your honor, Lord Janos. I'm denying its existence."
—*Tyrion Lannister*
played by Dominic Carter

Janos Slynt is the commander of the City Watch in King's Landing. Ned Stark thinks he and Littlefinger have bought him, but instead, Slynt arrests Ned, and King Joffrey appoints him Lord of Harrenhal. Tyrion, disgusted that Slynt orders Robert Baratheon's bastard children killed and has betrayed the previous Hand, quietly exiles him to the Wall.

The Kingsguard

Under King Aerys "The Mad King" Targaryen

- ❖ Lord Commander Ser Gerold Hightower "The White Bull" (died at Tower of Joy with Lyanna Stark)
- ❖ Ser Arthur Dayne, The Sword of the Morning (died at Tower of Joy with Lyanna Stark)
- ❖ Ser Oswell Whent (died at Tower of Joy with Lyanna Stark)
- ❖ Prince Lewyn Martell (died with Rhaegar on the Trident)
- ❖ Ser Jon Darry (died with Rhaegar on the Trident)
- ❖ Barristan Selmy (severely wounded with Rhaegar on the Trident), see below
- ❖ Ser Jaime Lannister (slew the King at King's Landing. Allowed Lannisters to kill Prince Rhaegar's family)

Under King Robert and King Joffrey

- ❖ Ser Barristan Selmy, Lord Commander of the Kingsguard

  Ser Barristan the Bold served under the Targaryens, then was forgiven and appointed to the Kingsguard by King Robert. Joffrey relieved him of service, over his protests, and Barristan left to go serve Daenerys, whom he recognized as the rightful heir. In the book he mentions he'd had suspicions Viserys was unfit, but after watching Daenerys, he recognizes her as Westeros's true queen.
- ❖ Ser Boros Blount
- ❖ Ser Preston Greenfield
- ❖ Ser Meryn Trant
- ❖ Ser Mandon Moore

  Ser Mandon is killed by Podrick Payne during the Battle of the Blackwater after attempting to murder Tyrion Lannister, likely on Joffrey's orders.
- ❖ Ser Arys Oakheart

  Ser Arys is sent to Dorne to protect Myrcella Baratheon.

❖ Ser Jaime Lannister "the Kingslayer" (raised to Commander of the Kingsguard when Barristan leaves)
❖ Sandor Clegane (appointed by King Joffrey to replace Ser Barristan)

Ser Ilyn Payne
"He hasn't been very talkative these last 20 years. Since the Mad King had his tongue ripped out with hot pincers."
played by Wilko Johnson
In the books, Ser Ilyn was captain of the guards for Tywin Lannister and joked that Tywin as Hand was the real ruler of Westeros: Aerys had his tongue cut out for the insult. King Robert made Ser Ilyn his new King's Justice when he married Cersei as a goodwill gesture to the Lannisters. He frightens most people, including Sansa. He is the one to execute Ned Stark, and keeps his sword Ice for a time.

Brotherhood without Banners
This is also the name of Martin's fan club, which throws parties for him at conferences.

Beric Dondarrion
played by Richard Dormer
In Season One, Ned Stark sends him to bring justice to Gregor "The Mountain" Clegane. When the War of the Five Kings begins, he takes on leadership of the Brotherhood Without Banners, soldiers who defend the land against all the marauding armies. Most of the scenes in Harrenhal contain mention of their deeds, an irritant to the Lannisters. It's eventually revealed that Beric has died multiple times, each time being brought back by Thoros of Myr.

Thoros of Myr
played by Paul Kaye
Thoros of Myr is a red priest, from the same religion as the red priestess Melisandre. In the book, he travels to Westeros when he discovers King Aerys' obsession with fire, while in the show, Melisandre mentions he was sent to convert King Robert.

Either way, King Robert liked him as he fought in tournaments with a flashy flaming sword coated in wildfire. Later, he joins the Brotherhood and discovers that after the dragons' return he has developed true powers…

Night's Watch

Lord Commander Jeor "The Old Bear" Mormont

"I'll not sit meekly by and wait for the snows. I mean to find out what's happening. The Night's Watch will ride in force, against the Wildlings, the White Walkers and whatever else is out there."

played by James Cosmo

Jeor Mormont is the Lord Commander of the Night's Watch. He ends season one by leading a great ranging north of the Wall to investigate sightings of White Walkers. He once led House Mormont until he took the black. Jeor's sister Maege and her daughters rule Bear Island.

Jeor chooses Jon Snow as his personal steward and is likely grooming him for command. When Jon slays a wight and saves him, Jeor gives him the House Mormont ancestral sword Longclaw. He is killed at Craster's holding when he loses control of his men and a fight breaks out.

Maester Aemon

played by Peter Vaughan

Aemon is the maester (healer, loremaster, and message-sender) at Castle Black. He was born Aemon Targaryen, great uncle (on the show, just uncle) to Mad King Aerys, though few remember his history. He's also the older brother of Egg (Aegon V) from the Dunk and Egg tales. He's about a hundred years old and blind. He, like other maesters, decides it's his duty to take no part in the War of the Five Kings. In Robert's Rebellion, he likewise stayed away from the fighting and let his identity vanish under his maester's chain. Samwell Tarly is assigned as Aemon's steward. See the Targaryen family tree on page 21.

Yoren
played by Francis Magee
This Night's Watch recruiter meets Tyrion when he visits the Wall. Yoren rescues Arya from King's Landing and escorts her north, disguised as one of his many boys. He defies Joffrey's soldiers when they come to kill Gendry, and he's killed for it in season two.

Ser Alliser Thorne
"You're boys, still. And come the winter, you will die...like flies."
played by Owen Teale
The Night's Watch Master-at-Arms is cruel and malicious. He's responsible for training new recruits and nicknames Jon "Lord Snow." He's crueler to Sam, whom Jon takes under this protection.

Samwell "Sam" Tarly
"I read it in a book"
played by John Bradley-West.
Samwell Tarly is the oldest son and former heir of Lord Randyll Tarly, the head of House Tarly. He thinks of himself as a coward and is relieved to become Maester Aemon's steward. He also becomes Jon's close friend and takes his oath beside him at the heart tree. At Craster's Keep. Sam falls for Gilly, one of Craster's daughter-wives.

Qhorin Halfhand
"So it is possible for someone to survive on their own out here?"
"Possible for the Halfhand" – *Jon Snow and Commander Mormont*
played by Simon Armstrong
Qhorin Halfhand is an experienced ranger scout, missing half his hand from a wildling battle. He leads a small scouting party including Jon north of the Wall where they capture Ygritte and Qhorin convinces Jon to kill him and turn spy in Mance Rayder's camp. He dies at the end of season two.

North of the Wall
Mance Rayder
"Mance was one of us once. Now he's one of them...we need to be more like them – do things their way." —*Qhorin Halfhand*
played by Ciarán Hinds
Mance Rayder, once a noted ranger of the Night's Watch, deserted his post and fled north of the Wall to become wildling leader and King-Beyond-the-Wall more than a decade ago. He's been recruiting nearly all the wildlings to stand united against the White Walkers. The Night's Watch regards him as a traitor and enemy threat. Though he's mentioned earlier, he first appears in season three.

Ygritte
"You know nothing, Jon Snow."
played by Rose Leslie
Lovely red-haired Ygritte fights for the free folk under Mance Rayder. She takes a liking to Jon Snow and expects him to show loyalty only to her as she offers to him.

Tormund Giantsbane
played by Kristofer Hivju
A Wildling leader under Mance Rayder, he commands Jon and Ygritte's assault on the Wall.

Craster
played by Robert Pugh
Craster is a disturbing ally who marries his daughters and has no sons. In fact, he sacrifices them to the White Walkers. After Commander Mormont, Sam, and the others are injured in battle they return to Craster's Keep. He's less than friendly, and is finally killed when his stinginess leads to violence.

Gilly
played by Hannah Murray
Craster's daughter-wife and pregnant with a son. Sam cares for her and attempts to rescue her on their first meeting. When he

returns to her home, she's giving birth to a son, doomed to be sacrificed by her father. They escape together, heading south for the Wall.

House Targaryen in Exile
Seat: Dragonstone and King's Landing (formerly)
Sigil: A three-headed red dragon on a black background
Motto: "Fire and Blood"
See the Targaryen family tree on page 21
Symbolism: The Celtic dragon was an ancient symbol of fertility, wisdom, and immortality. This creature was worn on kings' torques as a sign of royal rule. Druids revered the serpent and its counterpart the dragon as a source of healing, along with the egg-shaped stones they believed it laid. Daenerys finds the power within these stone eggs for herself, along with the power of divine rule.

Daenerys
"Not a queen, a Khaleesi."
played by Emilia Clarke
Daenerys was born to Queen Rhaella on Dragonstone, following the death of her father King Aerys at the end of Robert's Rebellion. Her mother died in childbirth and the king's Master-at-Arms, Ser Willem Darry, spirited Daenerys and her older brother Viserys across the sea. He eventually died, and with no protector, Viserys was called the "Beggar King" as he courted wealthy friends but had to sell all their assets including their mother's crown to survive. Viserys was abusive, but Daenerys's only protector. At last, Illyrio Mopatis arranged a marriage between Princess Daenerys and Khal Drogo. Drogo could provide ten thousand Dothraki warriors for Viserys to lead to Westeros.

Drogo gave his bride a stunning silver mare. In the book Drogo is more sympathetic toward his twelve-year-old bride; on the show, he's more brutal and terrifying. In both stories, Daenerys accustoms herself to being Drogo's khaleesi, and begins to claim power and determine her own destiny.

In Vaes Dothrak it's proclaimed that Drogo and Daenerys's

unborn child, the Stallion Who Mounts the World, will conquer all known lands. Daenerys loses Drogo and her unborn child when she trusts a Maegi to tend his festering wound, but she enters his pyre and emerges with her dragon eggs, hatched. From there, she travels to the city of Qarth on the edge of the Red Waste and then Astapor, Yunkai and Meereen in Slaver's Bay, seeking an army and ships to carry her to Westeros.

Viserys Targaryen
"You'll wake the dragon!"
played by Harry Lloyd
Daenerys's brother is brutal, with a noticeable trace of his father's madness. He is the one to teach Daenerys about Westeros before his death and she remembers him with conflicted feelings. When an angry Viserys sheds blood in Vaes Dothrak and threatens Daenerys, Drogo kills him by pouring molten gold on his head.

Khal Drogo
"A khal who cannot ride is no khal at all."
played by Jason Momoa
Drogo is khal of a khalasar of ten thousand. He comes to love and value Daenerys, helping her cultivate her independence. He sinks into catatonia at the hands of Mirri Maz Duur, and his funeral pyre awakens Daenerys's dragons.

Rhaego
Drogo and Daenerys's son. He was to be the Stallion that Mounts the World before he was killed before birth.

Ser Jorah Mormont
"There are times when I look at you, and I still can't believe you're real." –
Ser Jorah to Daenerys
played by Iain Glen
Jorah is a knight from Bear Island in Westeros and the son of Jeor Mormont, Lord Commander of the Night's Watch. Young, he married a greedy woman, Lynesse Hightower. He began

arresting poachers and selling them into slavery to pay his debts, as she could only be satisfied with great luxuries. He fled across the sea before Ned Stark, his liege lord, could arrest him. However, in the Free Cities, his wife left him for a wealthier man.

At Daenerys's wedding, Jorah offers his fealty to Viserys, and gives Daenerys several books of stories and histories about Westeros. Before much time has passed, however, he transfers his loyalties from dragon king to dragon queen. Originally, Jorah joins Daenerys as a spy for Varys, and passes along important information such as her pregnancy. However, Jorah comes to love Daenerys and turns his back on King's Landing despite the offer of a royal pardon.

See Ser Barristan the Bold (under King's Landing page 164)

Doreah, Jhiqui and Irri
"It is known"
Daenerys's handmaidens. Doreah, a trained courtesan, advises Daenerys and sleeps with her brother. In the book, she dies in the desert and Irri and Jhiqui follow Daenerys through all her adventures. On the show, Doreah betrays Daenerys with Xaro Xhoan Daxos and she leaves them both to die. Irri dies guarding Daenerys's dragons.

Aggo, Jhogo/Kovarro, and Rakharo
Daenerys's bloodriders. At the wedding, Drogo's bloodriders offer Daenerys fine weapons – a whip, an *arakh*, and a dragonbone bow – and, as per tradition, she gives them to her husband, protesting that she is only a woman. When Drogo dies, Daenerys offers Drogo's three greatest warriors, the "blood of his blood," these weapons and asks them to be her bloodriders. They refuse, as there has never been a female khal. When she emerges from the flames with her dragons, they kneel and pledge service. On the show, Rakharo is killed by a rival khal, but the bloodriders survive in the books.

Mirri Maz Duur
"Life must pay for life"
played by Mia Soteriou
The Lhazareen witch is a godswife who studied in Asshai and learned magic and prophecy. Khal Drogo's khalasar enslaves her and Daenerys saves her. As a reward, Mirri Maz Duur makes Drogo a healing poultice. On the show, she seems malevolent, but in the book, Drogo rips it off and ignores instructions, leaving it ambiguous whether it was poisoned or his own stubbornness dooms him. Regardless, Drogo's wound festers and he falls fatally ill. Daenerys asks Mirri Maz Duur to preserve him with blood magic. However, sacrificing Drogo's horse is not enough, and Daenerys's baby miscarries. Drogo lives but has no awareness, and Daenerys must sadly end his life. She binds Mirri Maz Duur to Drogo's funeral pyre and kills her, but also ironically proves Mirri's insistence that life can bring forth life – her sacrifices awaken Daenerys's dragons.

Dragons
The dragons are Viserion (white), Rhaegal (green) and Drogon (black, the largest and fiercest), named after her two deceased brothers and her late husband, respectively. In Qarth, Daenerys is given a crown decorated with three dragons in those colors. The dragons get progressively larger in each book, until they're rideable by the fifth one, if no longer especially tame…

Missandei
played by Nathalie Emmanuel
A slave of the free cities, she translates for Daenerys, though the khaleesi doesn't really need the help. Missandei also advises Daenerys on the local culture after the khaleesi frees her.

Grey Worm
played by Jacob Anderson
Grey Worm, the head of Daenerys's unsullied army, keeps the random name he drew from the pot the day she freed him (in the book), as he considers it lucky. He proves devoted to her.

Independent Characters

Illyrio Mopatis
played by Roger Allam
Illyrio is a Magister (merchant-lord) of the Free City of Pentos. The terribly rich and corpulent man arranges Daenerys's wedding to Drogo and conspires with Varys in the cells beneath King's Landing (where Arya overhears them). He is the one to give Daenerys the dragon eggs. In book four and five, more of his long-term schemes are revealed. He and Varys are both political planners manipulating the realm.

Ros
played by Esme Bianco
This prostitute begins near Winterfell and travels to King's Landing to work in Littlefinger's brothel. She appears in many key scenes. (In the books, the brothel belongs to Chataya, who has some of Ros' role. Ros is a combination of several book characters.) When she transfers her loyalty from Littlefinger to Varys, Littlefinger gives her to Joffrey, fatally.

Syrio Forel
"There's only one thing we say to Death...Not today!"
played by Miltos Yerolemou
Syrio Forel, Arya's "dancing instructor" sacrifices himself to save her when the Lannisters try to arrest her. His death isn't seen, and after Arya escapes, a second man from Braavos, the assassin Jaqen H'ghar, takes an interest and even kills three men for her. Since Jaqen H'ghar is a Faceless Man who can change his appearance, many wonder if they're the same person.

Jaqen H'ghar
"The Red God takes what is his, lovely girl, and only death may pay for life....speak three names and a man will do the rest."
played by Tom Wlaschiha
Jaqen H'ghar was languishing in the dungeons of King's Landing, before being dragged in a cage up to the Wall alongside

Arya. He and Arya are both captured by the Lannisters and taken to Harrenhal, where he helps her escape after promising to kill three people for her. Jaqen leaves Arya with a Braavosi coin and the phrase *"valar morghulis,"* all men must die. He is actually one of the Faceless Men of Braavos, a feared order of mysterious assassins with the ability to change their appearance at will. Intriguingly, in the book, he changes his face before leaving Arya, and his new face is soon seen interfering at Oldtown where the Maesters are trained. Since the Citadel has texts no one else possesses, Jaqen is likely trying to learn something... or prevent someone else from learning something.

Xaro Xhoan Daxos
played by Nonso Anozie
Xaro is a powerful merchant in the city-state of Qarth and one of the Thirteen who rule there. Daenerys travels there with her dragons and Xaro invites her to enter the city under his protection. She stays with him and he proposes marriage repeatedly. She needs wealth and ships to sail for Westeros, and Xaro offers her half the gold in his enormous vault in return for her hand in marriage...or for a dragon.

On the show, Xaro kills the Thirteen in his home and declares himself King of Qarth. With Pyat Pree, he steals Daenerys's dragons and hides them in the mysterious House of the Undying. After Daenerys retrieves them, she discovers her handmaid Doreah in bed with Xaro – she has betrayed Daenerys. Daenerys breaks into Xaro's vault, only to discover his great wealth is a lie. Daenerys imprisons Xaro and Doreah in the vault, and raids Xaro's house for enough treasure to buy a ship.

Pyat Pree
"When your dragons were born, our magic was born again."
played by Ian Hanmore
A warlock from Qarth and member of the Thirteen, Pyat Pree dwells in the mysterious House of the Undying in Qarth. The possessor of strange magics, he steals Daenerys's dragons and

takes them to the warlocks' stronghold, the House of the Undying. He tries to imprison her, and Daenerys's dragons kill him.

Salladhor Saan
played by guest star Lucian Msamati
Salladhor Saan, a pirate lord from Lys, commands a fleet of mercenary warships. He sails for King Stannis and provides him with thirty ships for the Battle of Blackwater, though he demands Queen Cersei as a prize along with vast riches. After the battle, Salladhor rescues the stranded Davos, but abandons Stannis's cause.

Qyburn
"Gods be good, Cersei, he rode with Vargo Hoat. The Citadel stripped him of his chain!"
played by Anton Lesser
At the beginning of season three, Qyburn is the only prisoner of Harrenhal to survive, and is discovered by King Robb and his company. Qyburn was a maester stripped of his rank for experimenting...in the book, his experiments were on living bodies, not just dead ones. He's rumored to have knowledge of black magic and necromancy. He also aids Jaime and manages to save his maimed arm. Qyburn accompanies Jaime to King's Landing, where he finds a new patron.

Places of the World

Asshai

Asshai is in the far south-east of the eastern continent, Essos, on the edge of the mysterious Shadow Lands, thus the city is called Asshai-by-the-Shadow. It is the origin of the Maegi, the Azor Ahai prophecy, and much dragonglass and dragon lore.

The Citadel

The Citadel of Oldtown, in Highgarden to the South, is where maesters are trained. Oldtown is the oldest city in Westeros. The oldest of lore books are stored there, and their leaders announce the changing seasons by sending a white raven.

The Crownlands

The Crownlands, King's Landing and nearby areas, are ruled directly by the Iron Throne. This includes Dragonstone and other islands in the Narrow Sea. The Crownlands are in the middle of the South: south of the Vale, southeast of the Riverlands, east of the Westlands, and north of the Reach and Stormlands. Bastards here bear the surname Waters.

Dorne

Dorne, the southernmost region of Westeros, contains the continent's desert, but also decadent water gardens, oranges, lemons, and fine wines. The land has a warm, exotic feel. Many of their citizens are descended from the Rhoynish people rather than the Andals, giving them darker skin and hair. Dorne only joined the Seven Kingdoms a century after the Targaryen invasion, and they maintain a degree of independence, still calling themselves "prince" and "princess." Bastards in Dorne are called Sand.

Dragonstone

The Targaryen family seat, an island settled by them before their scion Aegon the Conqueror arrived on Westeros. It's filled with dragon eggs, dragonglass, volcanic activity, and lost secrets yet to be discovered. Daenerys, like Aegon the Conqueror, was born there. It was the last Targaryen holdout during Robert's Rebellion, and Stannis had a long battle to capture and hold it. It's now Stannis's family seat.

Essos

The continent to the east, containing the Free Cities and the area around Slaver's Bay. Much of the inland area is taken up by the grasslands known as the Dothraki Sea.

Free Cities

The Free Cities, nine independent city-states, are located on the west coast of Essos: Braavos, Myr, Pentos, Volantis, Lorath, Lys, Tyrosh, Norvos, and Qohor. Braavos was founded by refugee slaves, while all the others are former colonies of the Valyrian Empire. Daenerys's wedding is held in Pentos, where Illyrio lives. Varys was born a slave in Lys, origin of some particularly nasty poisons. Robb's wife Talisa comes from Volantis, while the Blackfyres fled to Tyrosh upon their defeat. The Faceless Men train in Braavos.

The Gift

Brandon the Builder built the Wall, and Brandon's Gift is a stretch of land up to twenty-five leagues south of the Wall that pays its fealty and taxes directly to the Wall. Queen Alysanne the Good doubled this to fifty leagues, called the New Gift. Wildling raids have driven off many, and much of the land is abandoned today.

The Iron Islands

The Iron Islands off the western coast of Westeros include the islands of Pyke, Great Wyk, Old Wyk, and Harlaw. The soil is filled with stones and salt, but there are lead and iron mines here. The men of this land, called Ironmen or the Ironborn, are ruled by House Greyjoy of Pyke. They once ruled the Riverlands and much of the coast of Westeros before the Targaryen invasion. They pray mainly to the Drowned God.

The Lands of Always Winter
These lie far beyond the Wall, at the north of the known world. They're largely unexplored.

The Neck
This marsh-filled border between north and south in Westeros is ruled by the Crannogmen. While many call them poisoners, sneaks, and frog eaters, their House Reed has always proved loyal to the Starks.

The North
The North is the largest region, said to be ungovernable by any but a Northman. To the North, it's bordered by the Gift, the lands of the Night's Watch. To the South, its border is the Neck, the marshy choke point separating North from South. White Harbor is the major port city. The North is ruled by the Starks of Winterfell, formerly the Kings in the North. Bastards here are called "Snow."

Old Valyria
This mighty empire fell long ago, in a mysterious volcanic explosion known as the Doom. Today, only the Smoking Sea remains on its ruins, and travelers there rarely return. Much of their culture still remains, in the east where the Free Cities became independent after the fall and in the West, where the last great house of Old Valyria, the Targaryens, brought their culture, lore, and dragons.

Qarth
Beyond the Red Waste, the city of Qarth sits beside the straits that lead to the Jade Sea. Its prime position makes it the gateway between the lands of Westeros, Free Cities and Slaver's Bay, and more eastern lands. As such, it's fabulously wealthy and has been described as the center of the world.

The Reach
The second largest region, it is fertile and well-populated. This is the domain of House Tyrell of Highgarden. The Tyrells were stewards to House Gardener, the Kings of the Reach before Aegon's conquest, and inherited the lands after. They often fight Dorne, which is their neighboring kingdom, separated only by the Dornish Marches. Oldtown, where Maesters are trained, is the largest city. Bastards are given the surname Flowers.

The Riverlands
The Riverlands near the river of the Trident are ruled by the Tullys of Riverrun. This is a fertile area, but overrun by fighting in the War of the Five Kings. Harrenhal is the largest castle in the area, though in terrible disrepair. Bastards are named Rivers.

The Shadow Lands
At the eastern edge of the known world, the Shadow Lands beside Asshai are the source of dragon eggs. The Shadow Men, like Quaithe, cover their bodies in tattoos and wear red lacquered wooden masks. Some of them practice blood magic.

Slaver's Bay
On the site of the former Ghiscari Empire (rivals to Old Valyria), Slaver's Bay collects its wealth from the slave trade. Astapor, Yunkai and Meereen are the major cities. Their language is based in High Valyrian, and they continue to display the harpy symbol of Old Ghis. Daenerys reaches this area in season three.

The Seven Kingdoms
The Seven Kingdoms include Dorne, the North, the Reach, the Riverlands, the Stormlands, the Vale, and the Westerlands. The Crownlands and the Iron Islands are often included on this list.

Sothoryos
The Southern continent is a mysterious place of jungles and exotic creatures.

The Stormlands
House Baratheon rules the Stormlands from Storm's End, the castle King Robert bestowed on his brother Renly. It passes to Stannis, the last surviving brother. The Stormlands are south of King's Landing, bordered by the Sea of Dorne, Shipbreaker Bay in the east and the Reach in the west. Bastards here are called Storm.

The Summer Islands
The Summer Islanders in the Summer Sea, south of Westeros, are dark-skinned and skilled at archery.

The Vale of Arryn
The Vale, east of the Riverlands, is surrounded by the Mountains of the Moon. These are the domain of House Arryn, once called the Kings of Mountain and Vale. Their seat, the Eyrie, is so high in the mountains that it's considered unconquerable. Bastards are named Stone.

The Westerlands
The Westerlands are small, but filled with silver and gold mines. They are ruled by House Lannister of Casterly Rock, formerly the Kings of the Rock. The Westerlands are west of the Riverlands and north of the Reach. Lannisport, near Casterly Rock, is the chief town and port. Bastards here are called Hill.

Westeros
The continent of the Seven Kingdoms. The Narrow Sea separates it from Essos. Westeros is estimated to be about 3,000 miles from north to south and 900 miles wide at its widest point.

Yi Ti
Yi Ti on the Jade Sea sells spices and exotic goods that can make traders from Westeros rich forever.

A SONG OF ICE AND FIRE BIBLIOGRAPHY

A Song of Ice and Fire Novels

A Game of Thrones, Bantam Books, 1996
Corresponds to Season One. Encountering the White Walkers and finding the direwolves through Ned Stark's death.

A Clash of Kings, Bantam Books, 1999
Corresponds to Season Two. Renly, Stannis, Robb, the Iron Islands, and the Lannisters battle for the throne.

A Storm of Swords, Bantam Books, 2000
Corresponds to Seasons Three and Four. Tywin Lannister schemes in King's Landing while Robb's campaign begins to falter. Martin notes that book three offers

> Four weddings, *two* funerals, and a wake. Four trials as well. And three dragons, four bears, many mammoths, an unkindness of ravens, and a turtle of unusual size. More

battles, swordfights, and deaths than I can count, but two births as well, just to remind us all that life goes on.[78]

A Feast for Crows, Bantam Books, 2005
This book follows new and old characters to Dorne, the Maesters' Citadel in Oldtown, and Braavos, along with the Iron Islands. Cersei, Jaime, Brienne, Arya, Sansa, and Sam are viewpoint characters, along with some new faces; however, only half the usual characters appear, not including Tyrion, Daenerys, or Jon. Martin explains:

> When I was writing that book, it became so large that in 2003 or 2004 my editors and I realized that it would have to be split into two books. It wasn't finished at that point, but ultimately I made the decision to split the book geographically, since my characters were spread out across the world – to tell the story completely for some characters in *A Feast for Crows,* and to tell the story for some different characters, but within the same time frame, in *A Dance with Dragons.* In that sense, A Dance with Dragons is not the fifth book, but is more like four B. The two books run in parallel, and both begin five minutes after the end of *A Storm of Swords.*[79]

A Dance with Dragons, Bantam Books, 2011
This follows what the other characters – Bran, Jon, Daenerys, Tyrion and several Greyjoys – were doing during the events of book four, though this volume extends beyond that to rejoin Cersei's, Arya's and other characters' plots. Once again, several new individuals are introduced or become point-of-view characters. Much of the action takes place over the sea, rather than in King's Landing, as Daenerys prepares to move on Westeros. When Martin had first envisioned his seven book series as a trilogy, this was to be the title and possibly the plot arc of book two.

The Winds of Winter, Bantam Books, forthcoming
Martin has already released chapters from Arienne Martell, Victarion Greyjoy, Barristan Selmy, and Theon's point of views,

which he's read at various conventions. He adds that the sixth book will "open with the two big battles that I was building up to, the battle in the ice and the battle at Meereen – the battle of Slaver's Bay. And then take it from there."[80] He's also assured readers that we'll explore even farther north and discover what lies in The Lands of Always Winter. To the east, the Dothraki will also feature in the plot. In multiple interviews, he's mentioned uniting more characters as the plot threads from the East to the Wall interlock the characters' storylines.

A Dream of Spring, Bantam Books, forthcoming
This of course will conclude the epic struggle and wrap up the storylines. Of course, with an end to the saga, Martin could certainly have beloved characters find heroic or ironic deaths as their tales draw to a close. And he knows where it's all headed:

> The ending hasn't changed. I know the ending I'm heading for. It's like a journey and I know my eventual destination. I know the main roads I'm going to take to go there and the cities I'm passing through but I don't necessarily know all the fine details of the journey, that's what I discover along the way. You know, where I'm going to stop for dinner and what hitchhikers I'm going to pick up, where I'm going to hit a bump, where my car is gonna break down. So that's the sort of adventure of going on a journey or the adventure of writing a book. But I do know my ultimate destination.[81]

A Song of Ice and Fire Short Stories
Dunk and Egg

❖ "The Hedge Knight" (1998) available in George R.R. Martin, *Dreamsongs: Volume II* (Bantam Books, 2012) and *Legends I,* ed. Robert Silverberg (Ballantine, 2001).

❖ "The Sworn Sword" (2003) available in *Legends II,* ed. Robert Silverberg (Ballantine, 2004).

❖ "The Mystery Knight" (2010) available in *Warriors,* ed. George R.R. Martin and Gardner Dozois (Tor, 2010.)

❖ "The She-Wolves of Winterfell" Planned for inclusion in *Dangerous Women,* now delayed and instead intended for a forthcoming Dunk and Egg collection.

❖ *The Hedge Knight Graphic Novels* by Ben Avery and Mike S. Miller. (Dabel Brothers Publishing, Marvel. Ongoing.)

As described in the Dunk and Egg section of Targaryen history, these stories chronicle the future Aegon V, great-grandfather to Daenerys and the younger brother of Maester Aemon. He and Ser Duncan tour the countryside a century prior to *A Game of Thrones*. These popular tales brought Martin many new fans.

Other A Song of Ice and Fire Short Stories

"The Princess and the Queen" (novella about the Targaryen civil war called "The Dance of the Dragons"), *Dangerous Women*, ed. George R.R. Martin and Gardner Dozois. (Tor, 2013.)

Other A Song of Ice and Fire Adaptations

A Game of Thrones: The Graphic Novel Series by Daniel Abraham and George R.R. Martin, illustrated by Tommy Patterson (Bantam Books, Ongoing).

A Game of Thrones: The Board Game (Fantasy Flight Games, 2003). *A Game of Thrones: The Card Game* (Fantasy Flight Games, 2008). *Battles of Westeros* (Fantasy Flight Games, 2010). Many add-ons for all three games are available as well.

The Art of George R. R. Martin's A Song of Ice and Fire. Brian Wood & Patricia Meredith, Editors. (Fantasy Flight Games, 2005).

The Lands of Ice and Fire (Poster Map) George R.R. Martin (2012).

A Feast of Ice and Fire: The Official Game of Thrones Companion Cookbook. Chelsea Monroe-Cassel and Sariann Lehrer. (Bantam Books, 2012).

The World of Ice and Fire: The Official History of Westeros and The World of A Game of Thrones. George R.R. Martin, Elio Garcia, and Linda Antonsson. (Bantam Books, 2014).

INDEX

NOTES

1 George R.R. Martin, "Interview in Barcelona." *Asshai.com,* July 28, 2012. http://www.westeros.org/Citadel/SSM/Entry/Asshai.com _Interview_in_Barcelona.

2 "Correspondence with Fans," The Citadel: So Spake Martin, Aug 15 2001. http://www.westeros.org/Citadel/SSM/Category/C91/P90

3 "George R.R. Martin Interview," The World Science Fiction and Fantasy Convention, Aug 29-Sept 3 2012, in Chicago, IL.

4 George R.R. Martin, "The Hedge Knight" in *Dreamsongs II* (New York: Bantam, 2007), 607.

5 "Correspondence with Fans," The Citadel: So Spake Martin, Aug 15 2001. http://www.westeros.org/Citadel/SSM/Category/C91/P90

6 "A Very Long Interview with George R.R. Martin," *Oh No They Didn't.com,* Oct 10 2012. http://ohnotheydidnt.livejournal.com/72570529.html.

7 Linda Antonsson and Elio M. Garcia, Jr., "The Palace of Love, The Palace of Sorrow" in *Beyond the Wall: Exploring George R. R. Martin's A Song of Ice and Fire, From A Game of Thrones to A Dance with Dragons,* ed. James Lowder (USA: BenBella Books, Inc., 2012). Kindle Edition, Kindle Locations 354-357.

8 Bill Keveney, "In Game of Thrones, the Women Are," *USA Today,* Mar 29, 2012. Academic Search Complete, EBSCOhost.

[9] Myke Cole, "Art Imitates War," in *Beyond the Wall: Exploring George R. R. Martin's A Song of Ice and Fire, From A Game of Thrones to A Dance with Dragons* ed. James Lowder (USA: BenBella Books, Inc., 2012). Kindle Edition, Kindle Locations 1301-1306.

[10] Andrew Zimmerman Jones, "Of Direwolves and Gods," in *Beyond the Wall: Exploring George R. R. Martin's A Song of Ice and Fire, From A Game of Thrones to A Dance with Dragons,* ed. James Lowder (USA: BenBella Books, Inc., 2012). Kindle Edition, Kindle Locations 1773-1776.

[11] Martin, "Interview in Barcelona."

[12] George R.R. Martin, "The Mystery Knight" in *Warriors,* ed. George R.R. Martin and Gardner Dozois (New York: Tor, 2010), 668.

[13] Correspondence with Fans," The Citadel: So Spake Martin, June 3 2000. http://www.westeros.org/Citadel/SSM/Category/C91/P180.

[14] George R.R. Martin, "The Heirs of Turtle Castle" in *Dreamsongs: Volume I* (USA: Bantam Books, 2007).

[15] "A Very Long Interview with George R.R. Martin."

[16] Nick Gevers, "Sunsets of High Renown – An Interview with George R. R. Martin," *infinityplus.co.uk.* Retrieved Dec 2000. http://www.infinityplus.co.uk/nonfiction/intgrrm.htm

[17] Josh Roberts, "'Game of Thrones' Exclusive! George R.R. Martin Talks Season Two, 'The Winds of Winter,' and Real-World Influences for 'A Song of Ice and Fire.'" *Smarter Travel.* April 1 2012. http://www.smartertravel.com/blogs/today-in-travel/game-of-thrones-exclusive-george-martin-talks-season-the-winds-of-winter-and-real-world-influences-for-song-of-ice-and-fire.html?id=10593041.

[18] Antonsson and Garcia, "The Palace of Love, The Palace of Sorrow" Kindle Locations 316-317.

[19] John Birmingham, "A Conversation with Game of Thrones Author George RR Martin," *The Sydney Morning Herald.* Aug 1,

2011. http://www.smh.com.au/technology/blogs/the-geek/a-conversation-with-game-of-thrones-author-george-rr-martin-20110801-1i6wj.html.

20 Ibid.

21 James Hibberd, "EW Interview: George R.R. Martin Talks 'A Dance With Dragons,'" *EW.com,* July 12 2011. http://shelf-life.ew.com/2011/07/12/george-martin-talks-a-dance-with-dragons.

22 "Five Year Gap," The Citadel: So Spake Martin, Nov 30 1998. http://www.westeros.org/Citadel/SSM/Entry/Five_Year_Gap.

23 Hibberd, "EW Interview."

24 "A Very Long Interview with George R.R. Martin."

25 Nina Shen Rastogi, "TV's Best Show about Women," *Salon.com,* Apr 8 2012. http://www.salon.com/2012/04/08/tvs_best_show_about_women.

26 Sara Stewart, "Dames of Thrones," *New York Post,* March 26, 2013. http://www.nypost.com/p/entertainment/dame_of_thrones_7GGHhdZ30KagLzk4gfDbWI.

27 Jenna Sackler, "Women of Westeros: An Introduction to Feminism in Game of Thrones/A Song of Ice and Fire," *Feminists At Large,* Mar 14 2013. http://feministsatlarge.wordpress.com/2013/03/14/women-of-westeros-an-introduction-to-feminism-in-game-of-thronesa-song-of-ice-and-fire.

28 "A Very Long Interview with George R.R. Martin."

29 "Correspondence with Fans," The Citadel: So Spake Martin, Aug 15 2001. http://www.westeros.org/Citadel/SSM/Category/C91/P90

30 Gevers, "Sunsets of High Renown."

31 "Correspondence with Fans," The Citadel: So Spake Martin, Aug 15 2001. http://www.westeros.org/Citadel/SSM/Category/C91/P90

32 "A Very Long Interview with George R.R. Martin."

33 Roberts, "Game of Thrones' Exclusive!"

[34] "Correspondence with Fans," The Citadel: So Spake Martin, Aug 15 2001. http://www.westeros.org/Citadel/SSM/Category/C91/P90

[35] Hibberd, "EW interview."

[36] Rob Owen, "'Game of Thrones' has a 'Lord of the Rings' Connection," *Pittsburgh Post-Gazette,* April 17, 2011. http://www.post-gazette.com/stories/ae/tv-radio/game-of-thrones-has-a-lord-of-the-rings-connection-293758.

[37] Jim Vejvoda, "Who'd Win? Lord of the Rings vs. Game of Thrones," *IGN.* Nov 12 2012. http://www.ign.com/articles/2012/11/13/whod-win-lord-of-the-rings-vs-game-of-thrones.

[38] Antonsson and Garcia, "The Palace of Love, The Palace of Sorrow," Kindle Locations 330-333.

[39] Nick Gevers, "Sunsets of High Renown."

[40] "A Very Long Interview with George R.R. Martin," *Oh No They Didn't.com,* Oct 10 2012. http://ohnotheydidnt.livejournal.com/72570529.html.

[41] Robert Frost, "Fire and Ice," PoemHunter.com, 2003. http://www.poemhunter.com/poem/fire-and-ice.

[42] George R.R. Martin, "Slide Show" in *A Song for Lya and Other Stories* (USA: Babbage Press, 2001), 150.

[43] Jones, "Of Direwolves and Gods," Kindle Location 1740-1741.

[44] "George R.R. Martin Interview," The World Science Fiction and Fantasy Convention.

[45] Rowena and Rupert Shepherd, *1000 Symbols* (New York: The Ivy Press, 2002), 230.

[46] Padraic Colum, *The Children of Odin* (New York: Macmillan, 1920), 265. The Sacred Texts Archive. http://www.sacred-texts.com/neu/ice/coo/coo36.htm

[47] Sabine Heinz, *Celtic Symbols* (USA: Sterling Publishing Company, 2008), 71.

[48] Ibid., 129.

[49] Thomas Wentworth Higginson *Tales of the Enchanted Islands of the Atlantic* (New York: Grosset & Dunlap, 1898), 33-36.

The Sacred Texts Archive. http://www.sacred-texts.com/earth/teia.

50 Shepherd, *1000 Symbols* 182.

51 David Benihoff, George R.R. Martin, and D.B. Weiss, "Features: The Night's Watch," *Game of Thrones Season One* (Burbank, CA: HBO, 2012), DVD.

52 Ibid.

53 Ibid.

54 Ibid.

55 "Correspondence with Fans," The Citadel: So Spake Martin, Aug 15 2001. http://www.westeros.org/Citadel/SSM/Category/C91/P90

56 Joseph L. Henderson. "Ancient Myths and Modern Man," in *Man and His Symbols*, ed. Carl G. Jung (New York: Doubleday, 1964), 118.

57 Aniela Jaffé. "Symbolism in the Visual Arts," in *Man and His Symbols*, ed. Carl G. Jung (New York: Doubleday, 1964), 267.

58 Joseph Campbell with Bill Moyers, *The Power of Myth* (New York: Doubleday, 1988), 123.

59 Joan Gould, *Spinning Straw into Gold* (New York: Random House, 2005), 108.

60 Jones, "Of Direwolves and Gods," Kindle Location 1729.

61 Ibid., 98.

62 *The Voyage of Bran Son of Febal to the Land of the Living*, trans. Kuno Meyer (London: David Nutt, 1895). The Sacred Texts Archive. http://www.sacred-texts.com/neu/celt/vob/vob02.htm

63 Barbara G. Walker, *The Woman's Dictionary of Symbols and Sacred Objects* (San Francisco: Harper, 1988), 2.

64 Valerie Estelle Frankel, *From Girl to Goddess: The Heroine's Journey in Myth and Legend* (Jefferson, NC: McFarland and Co., 2010), 42.

65 Gould, *Spinning Straw into Gold*, 41.

66 Silvia Brinton Perera, *Descent to the Goddess* (Toronto: Inner City Books, 1981), 42.

67 Frankel, *From Girl to Goddess,* 22.

[68] Scott Meslow, "*Game of Thrones* Finale: The Powerful Women of Westeros," *The Atlantic,* June 20, 2011. http://www.theatlantic.com/entertainment/archive/2011/0 6/game-of-thrones-finale-the-powerful-women-of-westeros/240686.

[69] "Correspondence with Fans," The Citadel: So Spake Martin, Aug 15 2001. http://www.westeros.org/Citadel/SSM/Category/C91/P90

[70] Meslow, "*Game of Thrones* Finale: The Powerful Women of Westeros."

[71] Ibid.

[72] Shepherd, *1000 Symbols* 230.

[73] Correspondence with Fans," The Citadel: So Spake Martin, Mar 26 2002. http://www.westeros.org/Citadel/SSM/Category/C91/P60

[74] Clarissa Pinkola Estés, *Women Who Run with the Wolves* (New York: Ballantine, 1992), 4.

[75] Heinz, *Celtic Symbols* 131.

[76] Ibid., 137.

[77] Ibid., 75.

[78] Correspondence with Fans," The Citadel: So Spake Martin, June 3 2000. http://www.westeros.org/Citadel/SSM/Category/C91/P18 0.

[79] Rachel Brown, "George R.R. Martin on Sex, Fantasy, and 'A Dance With Dragons'" *The Atlantic,* Jul 11 2011, http://www.theatlantic.com/entertainment/archive/2011/0 7/george-rr-martin-on-sex-fantasy-and-a-dance-with-dragons/241738.

[80] Roberts "'Game of Thrones' Exclusive!"

[81] Gevers, "Sunsets of High Renown."

ABOUT THE AUTHOR

Valerie Estelle Frankel is the author of many nonfiction books:
- ❖ *Buffy and the Heroine's Journey*
- ❖ *From Girl to Goddess: The Heroine's Journey in Myth and Legend*
- ❖ *Katniss the Cattail: An Unauthorized Guide to Names and Symbols in The Hunger Games*
- ❖ *The Many Faces of Katniss Everdeen: Exploring the Heroine of The Hunger Games*
- ❖ *Harry Potter, Still Recruiting: An Inner Look at Harry Potter Fandom*
- ❖ *Teaching with Harry Potter*
- ❖ *Myths and Motifs in The Mortal Instruments*
- ❖ *Winter is Coming: Symbols, Portents, and Hidden Meanings in A Game of Thrones*

Once a lecturer at San Jose State University, she's a frequent speaker on fantasy, myth, pop culture, and the heroine's journey and can be found at http://vefrankel.com.

2874190R00110

Made in the USA
San Bernardino, CA
13 June 2013